STUDENT

CRITICAL DECISIONS:

CLARITY IN THE JOURNEY

Connect with God. Connect with Others.
Connect with Life.

LIFE
CONNECTIONS®
YOUTH

SERENDIPITY®
HOUSE

Critical Decisions: Clarity in the Journey
Student Book
© 2006 Serendipity

Published by Serendipity House Publishers
Nashville, Tennessee

ISBN: 1-5749-4343-X

Dewey Decimal Classification: 248.83
Subject Headings:
YOUTH \ CHRISTIAN LIFE

To purchase additional copies of this resource or other studies:
ORDER ONLINE at www.SerendipityHouse.com
WRITE Serendipity House, 117 10th Avenue North, Nashville, TN 37234
FAX (615) 277-8181
PHONE (800) 525-9563

1-800-525-9563
www.SerendipityHouse.com

Printed in the United States of America
13 12 11 10 09 08 07 06   1 2 3 4 5 6 7 8 9 10

CONTENTS

LIFE CONNECTIONS® YOUTH *EXPERIENCE*

Combine *teaching that engages a large-group* with dynamic *small-group experiences and discussions* and you end up grappling with reality and experiencing real life change. Throughout 13 sessions, small groups will find power in just being together and connecting.

 ## Get Ready

To get the most from this experience, spend some time with God each day leading up to your group session. Wrap your brain around the short Bible passages, listen to God, and jot down thoughts and insights.

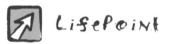 ## LifePoint

Your large-group leader will welcome everyone. You'll hear the "LifePoint" or big idea for the session, and then divide into small groups.

 ## Say What?

Enjoy fun, interactive experiences and discussions in your small group. Discuss the "Random Question of the Week" and join activities or discussions that lead into the session topic.

 ## So What?

The master-teacher will lead the entire group in understanding what God has to say on the topic. Content is deep, but engaging. Follow along, jot notes, and respond to questions in your book.

 ## Do What?

All study should direct us toward action and life change. It's easier and more helpful to discuss application in small groups. The goal is to be real with each other in order to connect with God and each other. Find power in the support and prayers of other students.

Now What?

To see real power in your life, you don't want to leave the session and just go on with life as normal. The "Now What?" assignments help you continue your journey and give you an opportunity to go deeper with God.

LIFE CONNECTIONS® YOUTH

AT A GLANCE

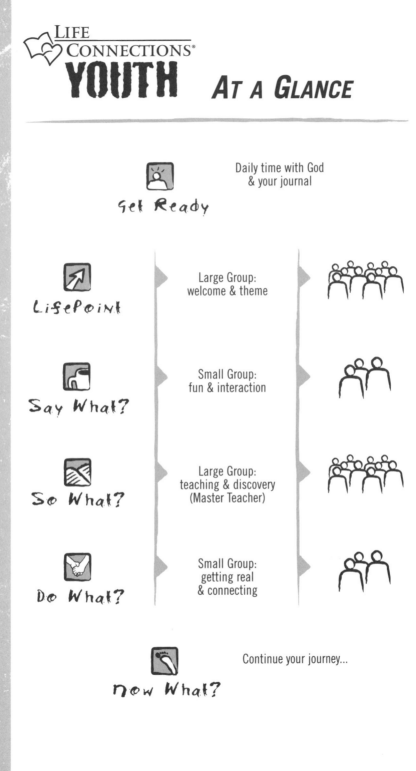

Get Ready — Daily time with God & your journal

LifePoint — Large Group: welcome & theme

Say What? — Small Group: fun & interaction

So What? — Large Group: teaching & discovery (Master Teacher)

Do What? — Small Group: getting real & connecting

now What? — Continue your journey...

GROUP COVENANT

It is important that your group covenant together, agreeing to live out important group values. Once these values are agreed upon, your group will be on its way to experiencing true Christian community. It's very important that your group discuss these values—preferably as you begin this study. The first session would be most appropriate. (Check the rules to which each member of your group agrees.)

☐ Priority: While you are in this course of study, you give the group meetings priority.

☐ Participation: Everyone is encouraged to participate and no one dominates.

☐ Respect: Everyone is given the right to his or her own opinion, and all questions are encouraged and respected.

☐ Confidentiality: Anything that is said in the meeting is never repeated outside the meeting without permission. *Note: Church staff may be required by law to report illegal activities.*

☐ Life Change: We will regularly assess our own progress in applying *LifePoints* and encourage one another in our pursuit of becoming more like Christ.

☐ Care and Support: Permission is given to call upon each other at any time, especially in times of crisis. The group will provide care for every member.

☐ Accountability: We agree to let the members of the group hold us accountable to the commitments we make in whatever loving ways we decide upon. Giving unsolicited advice is not permitted.

☐ Empty Chair: The group is open to welcoming new people at every meeting.

☐ Mission: We agree as a group to reach out and invite others to join us.

☐ Ministry: We will encourage one another to volunteer and serve in a ministry and to support missions by giving financially and/or personally serving.

1

THE REAL STORY

Spend a few moments getting to know God. Read one of these brief passages each day, and be sure to write down anything He reveals to you.

MONDAY

Read 1 John 2:15a

Are you a world-lover? What one thing that the world offers could you not live without?

TUESDAY

Read 1 John 2:15b-16

Think about "the world" not as God's creation, but as the systems and ideas that exist but are not of God. These systems and ideas are the schemes of our enemy, Satan. What are some of the distortions used by our enemy?

WEDNESDAY

Read 1 John 2:17

Ever been disappointed by something or someone that you thought you had to have? What did obtaining that individual or thing cost? How did the situation affect your relationship with God?

THURSDAY **Read 1 John 2:24-25**

By what standard do you make life decisions? Do you allow Christ to live through you, or do you try to do things your way?

FRIDAY **Read 1 John 2:26-27**

Whom do you trust for reliable advice? What role do God's Holy Spirit and Scripture play in helping you make right decisions?

SATURDAY **Read Titus 2:11-14**

How eager are you to do "good works" for God? Would those who know you consider you "sensible, righteous, and godly"? When Jesus comes back, where do you think He will find you? What do you think He will find you doing?

SUNDAY **Read 2 Peter 3:10-13**

What's your passion? Is it noble? Is it selfish? Describe the kind of person you should be as you wait.

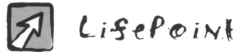 LifePoint

In order to grow into the godly men and women God intends for us to become, we must understand the nature of the world in which we live.

SMALL-GROUP
TIME:
Divide into
smaller groups of
4-8, preferably in
a circle. You will
have a small-
group leader for
"Say What?"

 # Say What? *(15 MINUTES)*

Random Question of the Week:
Why do the frogs in fairytales turn into princes but never princesses?

Group Experience: Cause and Effect
You will participate in an activity led by your small-group leader.

LARGE-GROUP
TIME:
Turn to face the
front for this
teaching time.
Follow along and
ake notes in your
Student Book.

So What? *(30 MINUTES)*

Building a Strong Spiritual Offense
1. What makes the offense of some football teams more successful than others?

2. How can you successfully make godly decisions?

Learning from the Bible

[LEADER] 15 Do not love the world or the things that belong to the world. If anyone loves the world, love for the Father is not in him.

[STUDENTS] Because everything that belongs to the world—

[LEADER] 16 the lust of the flesh, the lust of the eyes, and the pride in one's lifestyle—

[STUDENTS] is not from the Father, but is from the world.

[LEADER] 17 And the world with its lust is passing away,

[STUDENTS] but the one who does God's will remains forever.

[LEADER] 24 What you have heard from the beginning must remain in you.

[STUDENTS] If what you have heard from the beginning remains in you, then you will remain in the Son and in the Father.

[LEADER] 25 And this is the promise that He Himself made to us:

[STUDENTS] eternal life.

[LEADER] 26 I have written these things to you about those who are trying to deceive you.

[STUDENTS] 27 The anointing you received from Him remains in you, and you don't need anyone to teach you.

[LEADER] Instead, His anointing teaches you about all things, and is true and is not a lie; just as it has taught you,

[ALL] remain in Him.

Recognizing Worldly Strategies Opposed to God

3. More than ever before, we should realize that just because we can't see something doesn't mean it _____ _____ . Like germs attacking
   healthy bodies, _____ _____ _____ are daily attacking those
   who follow Christ.

Defining "the World"

4. How can living by the world's standards affect your determination to live by God's?

5. You can live in the world without being _____ by the _____
   _____ found in it.

Acknowledging the World's Strategies

6. What are three strategies the world uses to try to pull you away from God and His
   purposes for you?
   1.
   2.
   3.

7. What is the "lust of the flesh"?

8. What is the "lust of the eyes"?

9. What is "pride in one's lifestyle"?

SMALL-GROUP
TIME:
Small-group
leaders will
direct your
discussions.
Everyone will
gain more if
you are open
and honest in
responding to
questions.

 Do What? *(15 MINUTES)*

Group Experience: Looks Can Be Deceiving

1. I struggle with the "lust of the flesh"
   - ☐ A bunch
   - ☐ Sometimes
   - ☐ Hardly ever
   - ☐ I'd rather not say

   One thing I *feel* distracts me from my relationship with God is _____ _____.

2. I struggle with the "lust of the eyes"
   - ☐ A bunch
   - ☐ Sometimes
   - ☐ Hardly ever
   - ☐ I'd rather not say

   One thing I often *see* that distracts me from my relationship with God is _____.

3. I struggle with "pride in (my) lifestyle"
   - ☐ A bunch
   - ☐ Sometimes
   - ☐ Hardly ever
   - ☐ I'd rather not say

   One area of personal pride that distracts me from my relationship with God is _____.

LIFEPOINT REVIEW

In order to grow into the godly men and women God intends for us to become, we must understand the nature of the world in which we live.

"DO" POINTS

These "Do" Points will help you grab hold of this week's LifePoint. Be open and honest as you answer the questions within your small group.

1. <u>List secular values seen in TV and movies that illustrate the world's influence on our lives.</u> It's not difficult to identify the world's impact on culture when you look for it.
   How can you guard yourself against the negative influences of the media?

2. <u>Develop a monthly spending budget.</u> Money can be a great asset, or it can get you into trouble. The world says there's never enough. God says, "I want your heart."
   How will you invest your finances in such a way as to show your interest in living out God's values instead of the world's?

3. <u>Read God's Word daily to better understand our identity in Christ.</u> <u>Reading the New Testament reveals much about your new life in Christ.</u>
   What does the Bible say about how God sees you?

Prayer Connection:

Pray that each of you will be aware of the world's influences and will be spiritually strong in resisting them.

Share prayer needs with the group, especially those related to pulling away from worldly temptations in order to grow closer to God. Your group facilitator will close your time in prayer.

Prayer Needs:

Remember your "Get Ready" daily Bible readings and questions at the beginning of Session 2.

now What?

Take it to the next level by completing one of these assignments this week:

Option #1:
Keep a log of the TV you watch this week. List (1) the shows, (2) how much time you spend watching each one, and the (3) values each show presents (parents are silly, love is purely physical, commitment is old fashioned, dirty jokes are acceptable, do unto others whatever you want). How many schemes of the enemy have you identified in what you have viewed this week?

Option #2:
Set up a personal budget. Total all the money you receive each month from employment, chores, and allowance. Then take out ten percent for your church tithe and another small percentage to put in savings. The resulting amount is your discretionary income. Determine what you will do with it.

Bible Reference Notes

Use these notes to deepen your understanding as you study the Bible on your own:

1 John 2:15
love. The Greek word used for love in this verse is *agape*. It describes a love that is unconditional and committed. This is the same kind of love God shows His children.
world. The Greek word John uses here is *kosmos*, and it means that which is alienated from God and is contrary to who God is. It refers to a pagan culture that has abandoned God.

1 John 2:16
cravings. That part of human nature that demands gratification—be it for sexual pleasure, luxury, possessions, expensive food, whatever.
lust of his eyes. Greed that is aroused by sight. A person sees something and wants it. (For examples of this see Genesis 3:6; Joshua 7:21; and 2 Samuel 11:2–4.)
boasting. Pride in one's possessions; an attitude of arrogance because one has acquired so much. In its original Greek usage, this word referred to a man who claimed to be important because he had achieved so much when, in fact, he really had done very little.

1 John 2:17
pass away. To give oneself over to the love of the world is foolish because the world with its values and goods is already passing away (1 John 2:8).
lives forever. In contrast to those who live for the moment are those who give themselves to eternal, unchanging realities.

1 John 2:24
See that. John now issues a command. In the face of the lies of the antichrists they are to remain faithful to the Word of God.
what you have heard from the beginning. As an antidote to false teaching, John urges his readers to let the original message that they heard right from the start of their Christian lives control their perspective.
remain. John's point is that when they remain in the truth, they will remain in fellowship with God.

1 John 2:26
lead you astray. Those who left the church were not content to simply form their own fellowship based on their private doctrines. Instead, they actively sought to make converts from among the Christian community.

1 John 2:27
his anointing. The ultimate safeguard against false teaching is the Word of God. This is conveyed to our hearts by the Holy Spirit with whom we have been anointed.

NOTES

2

THE BATTLE ALONG THE WAY

Get Ready

Spend time getting to know God. Read one of these brief passages each day and spend a few minutes wrapping your brain around it. Be sure to jot down any insights you discover.

MONDAY **Read Ephesians 6:10-11**

How have you recently experienced the Lord's strength? In that situation, were you aware of the devil's attempts to interfere in your relationship with God?

TUESDAY **Read Ephesians 6:12-13**

Do you ever wonder why there is so much evil in the world? Do you find it difficult to resist the temptations the world presents? Describe one challenge you face in daily standing for Christ.

WEDNESDAY **Read Ephesians 6:14**

Do you feel that most of what you daily see, hear, and experience reflects God's truth? Picture yourself standing before God. How do your character and conduct measure up to God's standards?

THURSDAY **Read Ephesians 6:15**

Do you take the opportunities that God gives you to tell others about Jesus? What prevents you from sharing your faith with others?

FRIDAY **Read Ephesians 6:16**

Is your faith based on circumstances or does it consistently grow in spite of them? How do you respond to temptations? Is your faith in Christ strong enough to brush off the empty promises and ultimate discouragement that Satan throws your way?

SATURDAY **Read Ephesians 6:17**

Do you ever doubt God's power to carry you through *any* circumstance? How might better understanding and applying Scripture to your life help?

SUNDAY **Read Ephesians 6:18**

What do you pray for? Whom do you pray for? When do you pray? In your life, has prayer become a ritual or is it a passionate conversation with your Heavenly Father?

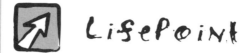 LifePoint

God gives you as a Christian everything needed to battle spiritual forces in the world.

SMALL-GROUP
TIME:
Divide into
smaller groups of
4-8, preferably in
a circle. You will
have a small-
group leader for
"Say What?"

 # Say What? *(15 MINUTES)*

2

Random Question of the Week:
What causes knuckles or toes to make that popping sound when you crack them?

Group Experience: "This Present Darkness"
1. How did what you hear make you feel?

2. Have you ever read anything like that before? If so, what did you read?

3. Did the reading remind you of any movies or TV shows you've seen?

4. Why do you think the author wrote about these things?

5. What kind of battle does this excerpt describe?

LARGE-GROUP
TIME:
Turn to face
the front for this
teaching time.
Follow along and
take notes in your
Student Books.

 # So What? *(30 MINUTES)*

Suiting Up
1. What makes an astronaut's helmet an essential part of exploring an alien planet?

2. Spiritual _____ requires equipment that only _____ can supply.

Learning from the Bible

[10] *Finally, be strengthened by the Lord and by His vast strength. [11] Put on the full armor of God so that you can stand against the tactics of the Devil. [12] For our battle is not against flesh and blood, but against the rulers, against the authorities, against the world powers of this darkness, against the spiritual forces of evil in the heavens. [13] This is why you must take up the full armor of God, so that you may be able to resist in the evil day, and having prepared everything, to take your stand. [14] Stand, therefore*

> *with truth like a belt around your waist,*
> *righteousness like armor on your chest,*
> *[15] and your feet sandaled with readiness*
> *for the gospel of peace.*
> *[16] In every situation take the shield of faith,*
> *and with it you will be able to extinguish*
> *the flaming arrows of the evil one.*
> *[17] Take the helmet of salvation,*
> *and the sword of the Spirit, which is*
> *God's word.*

[18] *With every prayer and request, pray at all times in the Spirit, and stay alert in this, with all perseverance and intercession for all the saints.*

Acknowledging the Spirit World

3. What is the theme of Ephesians?

4. What two things does Paul pray the Christians in Ephesus will receive?
   1. _____

   2. _____

Putting on Spiritual Armor in a Spiritually Dark World

5. True or False: The reason I struggle with my parents and friends is because of my attitude.

6. List the "full armor of God":

1.

2.

3.

4.

5.

6.

SMALL-GROUP TIME: Small-group leaders will direct your discussions. Everyone will gain more if you are open and honest in responding to questions.

 Do What? *(15 MINUTES)*

Group Experience: Ready for Battle

1. On a scale of one to five (with one being "I have no idea what I'm doing" and five being "I've mastered it"), how well have you mastered the use of each piece of spiritual armor?

Belt	1	2	3	4	5
Breastplate	1	2	3	4	5
Sandals	1	2	3	4	5
Shield	1	2	3	4	5
Helmet	1	2	3	4	5
Sword	1	2	3	4	5

2. Complete the following three statements:

One thing I need to do in order to be ready for the battle is _____

_____.

One thing I need to stop doing in order to be ready for the battle is _____

_____.

One thing I need to change in order to be ready for the battle is _____

_____.

3. Right now my prayer life could be described as
   ☐ Constant
   ☐ Spirit-filled
   ☐ Wishy-washy
   ☐ A valiant effort
   ☐ Nonexistent

LIFEPOINT REVIEW

God gives you as a Christian everything needed to battle spiritual forces in the world.

"DO" POINTS

These "Do" Points will help you grab hold of this week's LifePoint. Be open and honest as you answer the questions within your small group.

1. Memorize Scripture to help you deal with the temptations that trouble you most.
   Jesus used Scripture to combat Satan's 40-day onslaught. God's Word is the only offensive weapon you have.
   What do you need to do in order to increase your Bible study time?

2. <u>Create new friendships in order to share Christ.</u> God chose to reveal Himself to humanity through a relationship with His Son.
How can you win the right to be heard with a new friend so that you can tell them about your relationship with Jesus?

3. <u>Develop a prayer ministry to help you faithfully pray for the people God brings into your life.</u> Prayer is a powerful and often untapped spiritual resource for many Christians.
Do you ever forget to pray for others? How can you make prayer a daily priority?

Prayer Connection:

This is the time to encourage, support, and pray for each other.

Share prayer needs with the group, especially those related to areas in which you struggle—areas that keep you from being all God wants you to be. Your group facilitator will close your time in prayer.

Prayer Needs:

Remember your "Get Ready" daily Bible readings and questions at the beginning of Session 3.

now What?

Take it to the next level by completing one of these assignments this week:

Option #1:

Get out your current yearbook or borrow one from a friend. Turn the pages, identifying three students you feel do not have a relationship with Christ. Pray for each student. Then ask God to give you the opportunity to develop a friendship with at least one of them. (When the opportunity rises, make sure to take it!) Ask God to give you the time, place, and words to share.

Option #2:

Set a personal Scripture memorization goal. Choose verses suggested by a daily devotion you are reading, from the notes in your Bible, or ask someone for their favorites. Choose to memorize one verse a day. At the end of the week you will have memorized seven verses. At the end of the month you will have memorized around 30 verses. If you keep it up, by this time next year you will have committed at least 365 verses to memory!

Bible Reference notes

Use these notes to deepen your understanding as you study the Bible on your own.

Ephesians 6:10

be strong ... in his mighty power. Paul uses the same three words here as he used in Ephesians 1:19, when he first tried to describe God's indescribable power. In order to wage successful warfare against Satan, the Christian must draw upon God's own power. This is a power outside ourselves from beyond. This is not a natural power generated by the Christian.

Ephesians 6:11

Put on. It is not enough to rely passively on God's power. The Christian must do something. Specifically, he or she must "put on" God's armor.
full armor. Paul uses the Greek term *panoplia* (from which the English word "panoply" comes), which can be understood as the complete catalog of equipment needed by a soldier.
the devil's schemes. Evil does not operate in the light. It lurks in shadows and strikes unexpectedly, with cleverness and subtlety.

Ephesians 6:12

the rulers ... the authorities ... the spiritual forces. By these various titles, Paul names the diverse spiritual forces that rage against humanity. These are intangible spiritual entities whose will is often worked out via concrete historical, economic, social, and institutional structures. Part of the call to Christians is to identify the places where these evil powers are at work.

the powers of this dark world. It was no empty boast on Satan's part when, during Jesus' temptations, he claimed to be able to give Him "all the kingdoms of the world" (Matt. 4:8). These "world rulers" have real power, and even though Christ has defeated them, they refuse to concede defeat (though at Christ's second coming they will be forced to do so).

forces of evil. Another characteristic of these supernatural beings is wickedness. They are of the darkness, not of the light.

Ephesians 6:13

the day of evil. Although Paul may have in mind the final day of judgment, the immediate reference is to those special times of pressure and testing that come to all Christians, during which steadfast resistance of evil is required.

stand your ground. This is the second time Paul has spoken about standing fast (see also v. 11). Twice more, he will urge the same thing (vv. 13–14). This is the basic posture of the Christian in the face of evil: resistance. "Standing firm" is a military image. Paul may well have in mind the fighting position of the Roman legions. Fully-equipped soldiers were virtually invulnerable to an enemy onslaught—unless they panicked and broke ranks. As long as they "stood firm" when the enemy attacked, they would prevail in the long run. Most of all, their equipment, as will be seen in verses 14–17, was designed to enable them to "hold the position." This is the key to resisting evil.

Ephesians 6:14-17

All the pieces of armor (except one) are defensive in nature, rather than aggressive in intent. Each piece of armor is used by Paul as a metaphor for what the Christian needs to stand against the dark forces of Satan.

Ephesians 6:15

the belt of truth. This refers to the leather belt on which the Roman soldier hung his sword and by which he secured his tunic and armor (so he would be unimpeded in battle). The "truth" is the inner integrity and sincerity by which the Christian fights evil. Lying and deceit are tactics of the enemy.

the breastplate of righteousness. The breastplate was the major piece of armor for the Roman soldier. Made of metal and leather, it protected his vital organs. "Righteousness" refers to the right standing before God that is the status of the Christian, out of which moral conduct and character emerges.

feet fitted. These are the leather half-boots worn by the Roman legionnaire, with heavy studded soles that enabled him to dig in and resist being pushed out of place.

readiness. This term can be translated as "firmness" or "steadfastness," in which case "the gospel of peace" is understood to provide the solid foundation on which the Christian stands in the fight against evil.

Ephesians 6:16

the shield of faith. The large, oblong shield was constructed of layers of wood on an iron frame which was then covered with linen and hide. When wet, such a shield could absorb "flaming arrows."

flaming arrows. These were pitch-soaked arrows. Their aim was not so much to kill a soldier as to set him aflame and cause him to break rank and create panic.

Ephesians 6:17

the helmet of salvation. This heavy, metal head-covering lined with felt or sponge gave substantial protection to the soldier's head from all but the heaviest axe blow. Salvation is like that—but stronger, impenetrable. The sure knowledge that one's salvation is secure—that the outcome of the battle is already known—is the ultimate defense against Satan.

sword. A short, stabbing sword used for personal combat. The sword is the only piece of offensive equipment in the armor. The main task of the Christian is to withstand the onslaught of evil powers, not to attack, except in one way—by telling the Word of God in the power of the Spirit.

Ephesians 6:18

pray. Paul does not consider prayer a seventh weapon. Rather, it underlies the whole process of spiritual warfare.

in the Spirit. The Bible, the Word of God, is the sword of the Spirit. So, too, prayer is guided by the Spirit. This is, after all, spiritual warfare.

NOTES

3

THE MANY FACES OF THE JOURNEY

 Get Ready

3

Try to get alone with God for a few moments each day. During your time, read the daily passages and note your answers to the questions.

MONDAY   **Read James 3:13**

Do your friends come to you when experiencing relationship problems? Do you seem to understand the problems they bring?

TUESDAY   **Read James 3:14**

When did you last do something for someone other than yourself? When did you celebrate—without any thought for you—because of something good that happened to someone else?

WEDNESDAY   **Read James 3:15**

Do your attempts to make things better ever make the original problem worse? Do you give your opinion on a subject before anyone asks your advice?

THURSDAY   **Read James 3:16**

Would you say that you are wise or just a wise guy? When you consider your relationships, do most of them seem easy-going or full of conflict and unresolved problems?

FRIDAY   **Read James 3:17**

What adjectives would those who know you best use to describe the kind of friend you are? Could the words *gentle* and *merciful* be used to describe how you treat others?

SATURDAY   **Read James 3:17**

Are the motivations for your relationships pure or are you always thinking about how you can benefit from them? Do you treat some people differently than others? How would you feel if someone called you a hypocrite?

SUNDAY   **Read James 3:18**

Are relationships easy for you or difficult? Would you consider yourself a peacemaker? If so, explain.

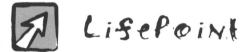

Healthy relationships that honor God don't seek the approval of "the world" but rely on the wisdom and peace of God.

SMALL-GROUP
TIME:
Divide into
smaller groups of
4-8, preferably in
a circle. You will
have a small-
group leader for
"Say What?".

 # Say What? *(15 MINUTES)*

Random Question of the Week:

What if "dog" was spelled C-A-T? Would it change anything?

Group Experience: Things in Common

Fill in the following without letting anyone know what you are writing. If you don't
have an answer for one of the questions, leave it blank.

My favorite food is_____

My favorite movie is_____

The best place to take a family vacation is_____

If I could play only one sport it would be_____

The most important meal of the day for me is_____

I get nervous when I_____

I study better when_____

The best pet is a_____

Family is_____

Someday I hope to make a difference in the world by_____

3

LARGE-GROUP
TIME:
Turn to face
the front for this
teaching time.
Follow along and
take notes in your
Student Book.

 # So What? *(30 MINUTES)*

Pick Me! Pick Me!

1. What one thing does everyone want?

2. With what two types of wisdom can people build relationships?

   1.

   2.

Learning from the Bible

[LEADER] ¹³ Who is wise and understanding among you?

[STUDENT] I am!

[ALL] He should show his works by good conduct with wisdom's gentleness.

[STUDENT] My bad!

[ALL] ¹⁴ But if you have bitter envy and selfish ambition in your heart, don't brag and lie in defiance of the truth.

[LEADER] ¹⁵ Such wisdom does not come down from above, but is earthly, sensual, demonic.

[ALL] ¹⁶ For where envy and selfish ambition exist, there is disorder and every kind of evil.

[LEADER] ¹⁷ But the wisdom from above is first pure, then peace-loving, gentle, compliant, full of mercy and good fruits, without favoritism and hypocrisy.

[ALL] ¹⁸ And the fruit of righteousness is sown in peace by those who make peace.

[STUDENT] Peace!

The Choice Is Yours
3. Everything I Say or Do Affects Others ...
     a. Positively
     b. Negatively
     c. Neither positively nor negatively
     d. Both positively and negatively

4. True or False: According to James, wisdom is knowledge.

Six Ways to Bring the "Wisdom from Above" Down to Earth
5. List the six aspects of godly wisdom James 3:17 mentions.
     1.
     2.
     3.
     4.
     5.
     6.

6. A person without integrity takes; a person with integrity _____. A person without integrity is always looking out for number one; a person with integrity looks out for the _____ of _____.

7. Having mercy means that you give someone what they _____, not what they _____.

8. True or False: Hypocrisy is one reason some people stop coming to church.

SMALL-GROUP
TIME:
Small-group
leaders will
direct your
discussions.
Everyone will
gain more if
you are open
and honest in
responding to
questions.

 Do What? (15 MINUTES)

Group Experience: Wise in Relationships

1. Which of the following best describes your relationship-wisdom?
   - ☐ I've got godly wisdom down to a science.
   - ☐ I try to act according to God's wisdom.
   - ☐ Sometimes I rely on God's wisdom, and sometimes I choose the world's.
   - ☐ I'm worldy wise; I know I need to work on changing that.

2. Which of the following describe you? You may mark as many as are appropriate.
   - ☐ I am a person of integrity.
   - ☐ I handle anger appropriately.
   - ☐ I care about others' feelings.
   - ☐ I am open to other opinions and ideas.
   - ☐ I try to show God's mercy regardless of how I am treated.
   - ☐ I treat everyone the same.
   - ☐ I am honest in my relationships.

3. In order to be a peace maker in the relationships in which God places me, I will...
   _____
   _____

Healthy relationships that honor God don't seek the approval of "the world" but rely on the wisdom and peace of God.

These "Do" Points will help you grab hold of this week's LifePoint. Be open and honest as you answer the questions within your small group.

1. Evaluate your relationship-wisdom according to the six aspects of godly wisdom. There is no better place to find help for your relationships than in the Bible. **What do you need to do to become wiser in your relationships?**

2. Seek forgiveness from those you have hurt. No relationship that has experienced a wrong can be made right until forgiveness is offered and accepted. **Has anyone hurt you? Whom do you need to forgive? Whom have you hurt? From whom do you need to request forgiveness?**

3. Ask God to empower you to be a peacemaker. Everything you say or do either creates strife or brings peace. **Pray that God will speak through your words and actions to bring peace into your relationships.**

Prayer Connection:

This is the time to encourage, support, and pray for each other.

Share prayer needs with the group, especially those related to changes you could make so that your relationships will reflect godly wisdom. Your group facilitator will close your time in prayer.

Prayer Needs:

Remember your
"Get Ready" daily
Bible readings
and questions at
the beginning of
Session 4.

now What?

Take it to the next level by completing one of these assignments this week:

Option #1:
Ask a mature, Christian friend to be honest about what type of friend you are. Ask them to answer the following questions about your friendship style:

Am I a person of integrity?

Do I handle anger appropriately?

Do I care about others' feelings?

Am I open to other opinions and ideas?

Do I try to show God's mercy regardless of how I am treated?

Do I treat everyone the same?

Do not comment on anything your friend shares with you, and don't get your feelings hurt. Simply take notes on what you're told. Prayerfully consider your friend's observations. Make a point to improve your relationships. This week, take at least one practical step to moving toward the person that God has designed you to be.

Option #2:
Meet your closest friends for breakfast, lunch, or coffee. Discuss how your friendships are reflecting God's wisdom. Evaluate the inclusive or exclusive nature of your relationships. Discuss how God can use your friendship with each other to point others to a Christ.

Bible Reference Notes

James 3:13

by his good life, by deeds. Understanding, like faith, is shown by how one lives. Specifically, understanding is demonstrated by a good life and by good deeds. This is what Jesus taught—and lived (see Matt. 7:15–23).

James 3:14

bitter envy. The word translated "bitter" is the same word that was used in verse 12 to describe brackish water unfit for human consumption. It is not applied to zeal (the word translated "envy" is literally *zelos*). Zeal that has gone astray becomes jealousy.

selfish ambition. The word translated here as "selfish ambition" originally meant "those who can be hired to do spinning." Then it came to mean "those who work for pay." It later came to mean "those who work only for what they get out of it" and it was applied to those who sought political office merely for personal gain.

in your hearts. This is the issue: What lies at the core of the person's being?

do not boast about it or deny the truth. Those whose hearts are filled with this sense of rivalry and party spirit should not pretend they are speaking God's wisdom. That merely compounds the wrong.

James 3:15

James uses three terms—each of which is less desirable than the previous one—to describe the true origin of this "non-wisdom." There is "earthly" wisdom that arises out of this world. There is "unspiritual" wisdom that arises out of the "soul" of the person. Neither form of wisdom is necessarily bad, except when it claims to originate with the Spirit of God or violates biblical principles. And then there is wisdom "of the devil" that is not neutral. This is literally, "demon-like"; i.e., that which is possessed even by demons (see James 2:19) or is under the control of evil spirits.

James 3:16-18

James contrasts the lifestyle that emerges from pretend wisdom (v. 16) with that which arises out of true wisdom (vv. 17–18).

James 3:17

pure. The Greek word describes a moral purity.

peace-loving. This is the opposite of envy and ambition. True wisdom produces right relationships between people, which is the root idea behind the word peace when it is used in the New Testament.

considerate. This is a very difficult word to translate into English. It has the sense of that "which steps in to correct things when the law itself has become unjust" as Aristotle put it.

submissive. True wisdom is willing to listen, learn, and then yield when persuaded.

full of mercy and good fruit. True wisdom reaches out to the unfortunate in practical ways, a point James never tires of making.

impartial. Literally, "undivided"; that is, true wisdom does not vacillate back and forth. It is the opposite of the wavering person in James 1:6–8.

sincere. True wisdom does not act or pretend. It is honest and genuine.

James 3:18

Peace flows from true wisdom in contrast to the sort of harsh insistence on "truth" that divides people. Those who sow peace reap right actions.

4

FINDING CLARITY

 Get Ready

Spend a few moments getting to know God. Read one of these brief passages each day, and be sure to write down anything He reveals to you.

MONDAY **Read Psalm 37:3**
Whom do you most trust? Does the relationship you have with that individual help you to be a better person? Explain.

TUESDAY **Read Psalm 37:4**
When is the last time you used the word *delightful*? Would *delightful* honestly describe your relationship with God? If not, what word would?

WEDNESDAY **Read Psalm 37:4**
What do you most want in life? What is your heart's desire? If God gave you your heart's desire, would you be delighted?

THURSDAY **Read Psalm 37:5-6**
Do you find it difficult to remain committed to something? What keeps you from making a commitment? In what ways does God honor your commitment to Him?

FRIDAY **Read Psalm 37:7**
What do you expect from God? Is what you expect worth the wait? How patient are you when waiting for God to answer your prayers?

Read Psalm 37:8

How do you feel when something good happens to someone else? Are you usually happy, or does it bug you that something good has happened to someone else?

Read Psalm 37:9

What are your hopes and dreams for the future? Do you ever get sidetracked from the plans God has for you because those around you seem to be having a great time without God?

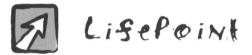 **LifePoint**

Some of the greatest moments in your relationship with God are those when you stop thinking about you, choosing instead to let your mind and body rest in time spent alone with Him.

SMALL-GROUP TIME:
Divide into smaller groups of 4-8, preferably in a circle. You will have a small-group leader for "Say What?"

 **Say What?** *(15 MINUTES)*

Random Question of the Week:

What is the difference between a toadstool and a mushroom? And if you were two inches tall, which would you choose as shelter?

Group Experience: Just a Minute

1. How do you feel when you have to wait on something or someone?

2. Where do you most often have to wait?

☐ Doctor's office
☐ Bus stop
☐ In traffic
☐ Online
☐ At lunch
☐ Other _____

3. What kind of "waiter" are you?

☐ Clock-watcher   ☐ Hand-wringer

☐ Leg-bouncer   ☐ Floor-pacer

☐ Nail-biter   ☐ Contented-sitter

☐ Eye-roller   ☐ "Fall-asleeper"

4. For whom would you most willingly wait? Number the following from 1 to 10.
(1 being the person to whom you would extend the most patience and 10 being
the person who would have you scowling at the clock.)

___ Professional athlete   ___ Friend

___ Coach   ___ School principal

___ Sibling   ___ Favorite relative

___ God   ___ Boyfriend/Girlfriend

___ Parent   ___ Medical professional

LARGE-GROUP TIME: Turn to face the front for this teaching time. Follow along and take notes in your *Student Book.*

So What? (30 MINUTES)

It's Not Fair!

1. What three-word cry is common to almost everyone?

2. What are five possible results of being overly concerned with what is and is not fair in the world?

1.

2.

3.

4.

5.

Learning from the Bible

3 Trust in the LORD and do what is good;
dwell in the land and live securely.
4 Take delight in the LORD
and He will give you your heart's desires.

5 Commit your way to the LORD;
trust in Him, and He will act,
6 making your righteousness shine like the dawn,
your justice like the noonday.

7 Be silent before the LORD and wait expectantly for Him;
do not be agitated by one who prospers in his way,
by the man who carries out evil plans.

8 Refrain from anger and give up [your] rage;
do not be agitated—it can only bring harm.
9 For evildoers will be destroyed,
but those who put their hope in the LORD
will inherit the land.

The Good, the Bad, and the Impatient

3. Psalm 37 contrasts the lives of the _____ with those who seek to live
   for _____.

4. What should you do when you notice a coworker chatting on his cell in the stock-
   room instead of working on the inventory?
   ☐ Tattle
   ☐ Watch and wait; the boss is sure to see him.
   ☐ Get back to work and let God take care of it.
   ☐ Pray that he'll get fired.
   ☐ Nothing. I'm talking on my cell too.

Worth the Wait

5. What does "delight in the Lord" mean?

6. What are the conditions of God's promise in Psalm 37:4?

7. What two things are you to do when you don't get what you want when you want it?
   1.
   2.

8. True or False: Waiting is a waste of time.

SMALL-GROUP
TIME:
Small-group
leaders will
direct your
discussions.
Everyone will
gain more if
you are open
and honest in
responding to
questions.

 Do What? *(15 MINUTES)*

Group Experience: How Do You Wait?

1. When you really want something, how many times a day do you pray to receive it?
   ☐ I don't pray
   ☐ Once
   ☐ Twice
   ☐ Three times
   ☐ More than three times a day

2. When life seems great and you don't really need anything, how many times a day do you pray?
   ☐ I don't pray every day
   ☐ Once
   ☐ Twice
   ☐ Three times
   ☐ More than three times a day

3. How do you usually react to unfair situations? Check all that apply.
- ☐ I become angry and agitated.
- ☐ I continue to do good things for God.
- ☐ I trust in God's justice.
- ☐ I complain to anyone who will listen.
- ☐ I silently and expectantly wait before the Lord.

4. What is the most difficult thing about waiting on God? What is the greatest benefit?

LIFEPOINT
REVIEW

Some of the greatest moments in your relationship with God are those when you stop thinking about you, choosing instead to let your mind and body rest in time spent alone with Him.

"DO" POINTS

These "Do" Points will help you grab hold of this week's LifePoint. Be open and honest as you answer the questions within your small group.

1. Prioritize your passions according to God's standards. You will lose interest in the things you love most if you allow them to come before God. God alone brings meaning and fulfillment.
   How can you use the things you love most for God?

2. Be faithful to do the little things while waiting for bigger things to come. Great accomplishments for God result from faithfulness to the daily opportunities He provides.
   Why does it seem more important to tackle great things for God rather than investing in daily tasks that serve Him and others?

3. Tell others about how God gives you your heart's desires. One way you can encourage people and glorify God is by telling others of God's blessings on your life.
   When is the last time you told someone about God's blessings?

Prayer Connection:

Share prayer needs with the group, especially those related to your concern with the unfairness in the world and delighting in God in spite of it. Your group facilitator will close your time in prayer.

Prayer Needs:

Remember your "Get Ready" daily Bible readings and questions at the beginning of Session 5.

 now What?

Take it to the next level by completing one of these assignments this week:

Option #1:
List the ten things you love most. Post the list where you will see it every day. Tape it on your bathroom mirror or inside your locker at school. At the end of the week, determine how the items on your list fit into God's plan for your life. Mark off things that might keep you from being the person God wants you to be.

Option #2:
Specifically choose three acts of service that you can do to minister to others this week. Choose things that will keep you from receiving public recognition. If you can serve in secret, all the better. At the end of the week, evaluate how each of the things you did made you feel. Ask God to continue to use you to serve others as He prepares you for your future with Him.

Bible Reference notes

Use these notes to deepen your understanding as you study the Bible on your own:

Psalm 37:3   ***trust in the LORD.*** This is a deep reliance on the God who promises to punish the ungodly and reward the righteous.
the land. Many interpreters see Israel's promised land as a type of heaven (John 14:1–6).
enjoy safe pasture. God's people are often analogized as sheep, with Jesus as the Shepherd (John 10:27–29).

Psalm 37:4   Men and women who delight in God desire only what will please Him. The desires mentioned here are not casual wishes but rather innermost desires.
heart. This refers to the center of the human spirit that produces emotions, thought, motivations, courage, and action (see Prov. 4:23).

Psalm 37:5   ***Commit your way.*** This, literally, means "to roll it over on" the Lord. God's people can place the weight of life upon the Lord (see Phil. 4:6–7).

Psalm 37:6   ***noonday sun.*** No shade of reproach or sin will remain.

Psalm 37:7   ***Be still ... wait patiently.*** To hush the spirit and to be silent before the Lord, knowing that God's timing is never wrong.

Psalm 37:8   ***do not fret.*** God's goodness is more evident in how He works through our troubles and defeats than in the successes of the wicked.

NOTES

NOTES

THE WAY OF THE JOURNEY

 Get Ready

Spend a few moments getting to know God. Read one of these brief passages each day, and be sure to write down anything He reveals to you.

MONDAY   **Read Philippians 2:5**

Do you ever have a bad attitude? If so, what causes it? What adjustments can you make to have a more like Christ-like attitude?

TUESDAY   **Read Philippians 2:6-7**

Have you ever acted super-spiritual? How should knowing that Jesus temporarily gave up His place in heaven impact the way you live?

WEDNESDAY   **Read Philippians 2:8**

Are you an obedient person? How far would you go to obey God? What would you be willing to sacrifice for Him?

THURSDAY

Read Philippians 2:9

What kind of obedience and devotion does God require of you? Do you expect God to reward you for your loyalty? If so, with what do you think He will reward you?

FRIDAY

Read Philippians 2:10

Do you think of Jesus more as a buddy or as the Lord? How do you think each helps your relationship with Him? How do you show Him respect and honor?

SATURDAY

Read Philippians 2:11

Is it natural for you to tell others about Christ? When you share your faith, do people take you seriously? In what ways—other than giving verbal testimony—do you acknowledge Christ as Lord of your life?

SUNDAY

Read Philippians 2:11

In addition to claiming Jesus as Lord of your life, do you also profess Him as Lord of heaven and earth? How does this truth influence the way you view the world?

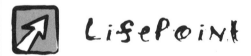 LifePoiNt

Surrendering your life to God's will means living by His values instead of the world's.

Say What? (15 MINUTES)

Random Question of the Week:

Why are the sand dollars that wash up on the beach almost always broken?

Group Experience: Who Knows?

1. How do clues help us find answers?

2. If you could have the answer to one particularly big question (such as whom you will marry), how might it change your life?

3. How would knowing God's will for you affect what you are doing and the plans you are making for the future?

LARGE-GROUP
TIME:
Turn to face
the front for this
teaching time.
Follow along and
take notes in your
Student Book.

 # So What? *(30 MINUTES)*

The Search for God's Will

1. How does the search for God's will seem like a trek down Dorothy's yellow brick road?

2. True or False: Following God's will is much easier when you understand what God's will is.

Learning from the Bible

⁵ Make your own attitude that of Christ Jesus,
⁶ who, existing in the form of God, did not
consider equality with God
as something to be used for His own
advantage.
⁷ Instead He emptied Himself by assuming the
form of a slave,
taking on the likeness of men.
And when He had come as a man in His
external form,
⁸ He humbled Himself by becoming obedient
to the point of death—even to death on a cross.
⁹ For this reason God also highly exalted Him
and gave Him the name that is above every
name,
¹⁰ so that at the name of Jesus every knee should
bow—
of those who are in heaven and on earth and
under the earth—
¹¹ and every tongue should confess that Jesus
Christ is Lord,
to the glory of God the Father.

What Is God's Will?

3. God's will is simply what God desires for you to _____
and _____.

4. God's will is not _____.

Jesus' Example of How to Live in the Will of God and Make Wise Decisions

5. List three ways Jesus showed us how to live in the will of God and make wise decisions.

    1.

    2.

    3.

6. What was Jesus' response to those who wanted to make Him their king?

   ☐ He accepted and was crowned King of the Jews

   ☐ He preached a sermon on "The One True King"

   ☐ He went to a mountain by Himself

   ☐ He rebuked the people

7. Jesus knew that it was far more important to follow God's will than to ...

   ☐ Please Himself

   ☐ Please Peter

   ☐ Please people

   ☐ All of the above

SMALL-GROUP
TIME:
Small-group
leaders will
direct your
discussions.
Everyone will
gain more if
you are open
and honest in
responding to
questions.

Do What? (15 MINUTES)

Group Experience: Like Christ

1. If you were in Jesus' shoes, which of the following would be most difficult for you?
   - ☐ Not using my divine power as a free pass to do things my way (v.6)
   - ☐ Humbling myself (v. 7,8)
   - ☐ Acting as a servant (v. 7)
   - ☐ Looking like any average human (v. 7)
   - ☐ Obeying God's will to the point of death (v. 8)

2. What is it about your character that makes it difficult to be like God wants you to be?

3. What is it about your conduct that makes it difficult for you to do what God wants you to do?

Surrendering your life to God's will means living by His values instead of the world's.

These "Do" Points will help you grab hold of this week's LifePoint. Be open and honest as you answer the questions within your small group.

1. List three things that threaten your loyalty to Christ. Many things can come between you and your relationship with Jesus.
   What persons, possessions, or obsessions are turning your loyalty away from Christ?

2. This week, keep a journal of the difficult choices you make. Some choices are simple but others are difficult to make on your own.
   What is the most difficult choice you're facing? How will it impact you and those you care about?

3. Pray for discernment in making the right choices. Sometimes you may make a good choice but not always the best one.
   How will you be able to determine whether or not you have made the best possible choice?

Prayer Connection:

This is the time to encourage, support, and pray for each other.

Share prayer needs with the group, especially those related to struggles in following God's will for you. Your group facilitator will close your time in prayer.

Prayer Needs:

Remember your
"Get Ready" daily
Bible readings
and questions at
the beginning of
Session 6.

 # now What?

Take it to the next level by completing one of these assignments this week:

Option #1:

Make a "First Will and Testament." List the personal resources you are willing to commit to God's use. Include time, talents, personal finances, and anything else that you can offer God. Use wording similar to, "Today (insert date) I give to God my (list resources) to be used by Him in anyway He decides." Sign it and have two mature Christians sign as witnesses to your commitment. Keep your "will" accessible so that you can measure your faithfulness to the commitments.

Option #2:

Copy Philippians 2:5-11 in your own handwriting every day this week. (No typing: that's cheating.) Each day, underline the quality of Christ that you find most difficult to imagine Him doing; circle the quality of Christ that you would most like to have; and complete the sentence, "My attitude is …".

Bible Reference Notes

Use these notes to deepen your understanding as you study the Bible on your own.

Philippians 2:6-11

There is little agreement between scholars as to how this hymn breaks into verses or how it is to be phrased. However, one thing is clear. The hymn has two equal parts. Part one (vv. 6–8) focuses on the self-humiliation of Jesus. Part two (vv. 9–11) focuses on God's exaltation of Jesus. In part one, Jesus is the subject of the two main verbs, while in part two God is the subject of the two main verbs.

Philippians 2:6

being. This is not the normal Greek word for "being." This word carries the idea of preexistence. By using it, Paul is saying Jesus always existed in the form of God.

very nature. The Greek word is *morphe* (used twice by Paul in this hymn). He says Jesus was "in very nature God," and He then took upon Himself "the very nature of a servant." This is a key word in understanding the nature of Christ.

to be grasped. This is a rare word, used only at this point in the New Testament. It refers to the fact that Jesus did not have to "snatch" equality with God. Equality was not something He needed to acquire. It was His already, and He could give it away. Giving, not grasping, is what Jesus did.

Philippians 2:7

made himself nothing. Literally, "to empty," or "to pour out until the container is empty."

taking the very nature of a servant. Jesus gave up Godhood and took on slavehood. From being the ultimate master, He became the lowest servant. He left ruling for serving.

being made. In contrast to the verb in verse 6 (that stresses Christ's eternal nature), this verb points to the fact that at a particular time He was born in the likeness of a human being.

human likeness. Jesus did not just seem to be human. He assumed the identity and flesh of a human being and was similar in all ways to other human beings.

Philippians 2:8

in appearance as a man. The word translated "in appearance" is *schema* and denotes that which is outward and changeable (distinct from *morphe*, which denotes that which is essential and eternal).

he humbled himself. This is the central point of one who lived a life of self-sacrifice, self-renunciation, and self-surrender.

obedient to death. The extent of this humbling is defined by this clause. Jesus humbled Himself to the furthest point one can go. He submitted to death itself for the sake of both God and humanity. There was not a more dramatic way to demonstrate humility.

death on a cross. This was no ordinary death. Crucifixion was a harsh, demeaning, and utterly painful way to die. According to the Old Testament, those who died by hanging on a tree were considered to have been cursed by God.

Philippians 2:9

name. In the ancient world, a name was more than just a way of distinguishing one individual from another. It revealed the inner nature or character of a person. The name given the resurrected Jesus is the supreme name—the name above all names—because this is Jesus' identity in His innermost being.

Philippians 2:10

bow. Everyone will one day pay homage to Jesus. This worship will come from all of creation—all angels (in heaven), all people (on earth), and all demons (under the earth).

Philippians 2:11

Jesus Christ is Lord. The climax of this hymn. This is the earliest and most basic confession of faith on the part of the church (see Acts 2:36; Rom. 10:9; 1 Cor. 12:3).

Lord. This is the name that was given to Jesus; the name that reflects who He really is (see v. 9). This is the name of God. Jesus is the supreme Sovereign of the universe.

5

NOTES

Session

6

THE WRONG WAY

 **Get Ready**

Spend a few moments getting to know God. Read one of these brief passages each day, and be sure to write down anything He reveals to you.

MONDAY

Read Hebrews 12:1

What keeps you from being effective in your witness for Christ? What sins hurt your relationship with God? Have you confessed them? If so, why do you think they keep tripping you up?

TUESDAY

Read Hebrews 12:2

What motivates the things you do, the things you say, and the relationships you pursue? How obvious is your devotion to Christ to others?

WEDNESDAY

Read Hebrews 12:3

Do you ever get tired of living the way God expects you to? Do you think Jesus ever grew weary of fulfilling His purpose on earth? How does Jesus' example encourage you to follow God in spite of circumstances?

THURSDAY   **Read Hebrews 12:4**

What has resisting temptation cost you? What was the most difficult spiritual strug-gle you ever experienced? What was the outcome of that situation?

FRIDAY   **Read Hebrews 12:5-8**

Do you ever feel like a child of God? What have you done that has resulted in God's discipline? What form has His discipline taken?

SATURDAY   **Read Hebrews 12:9-10**

How do your parents discipline you? When is the last time they did? How do you respond to discipline?

SUNDAY   **Read Hebrews 12:11**

Can you remember a time when you actually felt blessed when disciplined? How has discipline benefited you?

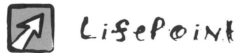 LifePoint

In order to receive His grace and forgiveness when we sin, we must respond to God through confession and repentance.

SMALL-GROUP
TIME:
Divide into
smaller groups of
4-8, preferably in
a circle. You will
have a small-
group leader for
"Say What?"

 # Say What? *(20 MINUTES)*

Random Question of the Week:
Why do fans *sit* in the *stands* at a football game?

Group Experience: Coming Clean
1. What sins are most visible? Which are easiest to keep hidden?

2. When are you most aware of the sin in your life?

3. What decisions result from your awareness of sin?

G

LARGE-GROUP
TIME:
Turn to face
the front for this
teaching time.
Follow along and
take notes in your
Student Book.

So What? *(30 MINUTES)*

Rules, Rules, Rules
1. What is one thing your parents do that reflects God's role in your life?

2. List three things related to following directions that you can count on:
    1.
    2.
    3.

Learning from the Bible

[1] Therefore since we also have such a large cloud of witnesses surrounding us, let us lay aside every weight and the sin that so easily ensnares us, and run with endurance the race that lies before us, [2] keeping our eyes on Jesus, the source and perfecter of our faith, who for the joy that lay before Him endured a cross and despised the shame, and has sat down at the right hand of God's throne.

[3] For consider Him who endured such hostility from sinners against Himself, so that you won't grow weary and lose heart. [4] In struggling against sin, you have not yet resisted to the point of shedding your blood. [5] And you have forgotten the exhortation that addresses you as sons:

> My son, do not take the Lord's discipline lightly,
> or faint when you are reproved by Him;
> [6] for the Lord disciplines the one He loves,
> and punishes every son whom He receives.

[7] Endure it as discipline: God is dealing with you as sons. For what son is there whom a father does not discipline? [8] But if you are without discipline—which all receive—then you are illegitimate children and not sons. [9] Furthermore, we had natural fathers discipline us, and we respected them. Shouldn't we submit even more to the Father of spirits and live? [10] For they disciplined us for a short time based on what seemed good to them, but He does it for our benefit, so that we can share His holiness. [11] No discipline seems enjoyable at the time, but painful. Later on, however, it yields the fruit of peace and righteousness to those who have been trained by it.

What the Bible Says about Sin

3. Check the statements that help define sin:
   ☐ Missing the mark of God's righteousness
   ☐ Thinking, saying, or doing something that is not in God's plan for you
   ☐ Hitting the bull's eye
   ☐ Missing the mark of God's holiness

4. True or False? Romans 6:23 says that the penalty of sin is loneliness.

5. List four things, outside the promise of eternal life, that sin affects.
   1.
   2.
   3.
   4.

God's Response to Sin

6. For what two reasons does God want you to completely avoid sin?
   1.
   2.

7. How does God show His love to you?

8. True or False: God turns all of your experiences into growth opportunities.

Your Response to God

9. According to Hebrews 12:1, what are we supposed to do with sin?
   ☐ Trust God to make it go away.
   ☐ Ignore it.
   ☐ Lay it aside.
   ☐ Embrace it.

10. What are the two parts of true repentance?
    1.
    2.

SMALL-GROUP
TIME:
Small-group
leaders will
direct your
discussions.
Everyone will
gain more if
you are open
and honest in
responding to
questions.

Do What? *(15 MINUTES)*

Group Experience: Weighed Down

1. How did the additional weight affect the strength of his legs?

2. How might the books represent sin?

3. How did his endurance represent resisting temptation?

4. What sins are keeping you giving your best for God?

**LIFEPOINT
REVIEW**

In order to receive His grace and forgiveness when we sin, we must respond to God through confession and repentance.

"DO" POINTS

These "Do" Points will help you grab hold of this week's LifePoint. Be open and honest as you answer the questions within your small group.

1. <u>Confess to God the sins in your life.</u> Don't try to hide anything from Him. God knows your thoughts.
   What specific sins do you need to confess? Do any of them keep showing back up in your life, even though you've repeatedly given them over to God?

2. <u>Accept God's forgiveness for sins committed this week.</u> If you confess your sins—any and all sins—God will forgive you.
   Do you have a difficult time accepting God's forgiveness? If so, is it because you feel unworthy or because you doubt God's promises?

3. <u>Ask a trusted, mature Christian to pray with you about the sin with which you most struggle.</u> God places people in your life to help you deal with the things that are bigger than you are. Sin is bigger than all of us, but we can find strength and accountability in each other.
   Who you will you contact to be your prayer partner?

Prayer Connection:

This is the time to encourage, support, and pray for each other as you confront and confess the sin in your life. Remember, true repentance brings God's forgiveness.

Share prayer needs with the group, especially those related to personal sin and repentance. Your group facilitator will close your time in prayer.

Prayer Needs:

Remember your "Get Ready" daily Bible readings and questions at the beginning of Session 7.

now What?

Take it to the next level by completing the "Now What?" assignment this week:

Neatly fold a piece of paper so it's easy to carry with you. Place it in a book at school, a Bible, or keep it neatly folded in your pocket or purse. During the week, tear the paper each time you become aware of a sin in your life. Then fold it and return it to your pocket, purse, or book. At the end of the week, note the number of tears in the paper. Ask yourself, *If the paper represents my relationship with God and the tears represent sin in my life, what must my relationship with God look like after seven days?* (Remember God's promise to forgive you of your sin.)

Bible Reference Notes

Use these notes to deepen your understanding as you study the Bible on your own:

Hebrews 12:1

witnesses. This is the same word as the one for "martyrs." It is probably a deliberate play on words in which both meanings are intended. The heroes of faith are pictured as a cheering section of former runners, urging contemporary runners to keep on as they did.

throw off everything. In Greek games at the time, runners ran naked so that no clothes would hinder their movement.

the sin that so easily entangles. Just as a flowing robe makes it impossible to run, so sin prevents one from pursuing Christ.

Hebrews 12:2

fix our eyes on Jesus. In races of the time, the prize for the race was placed at the end to motivate the runners. Jesus is here described as the prize upon which we are to focus.

joy set before him. Jesus knew the joy His mission of reconciliation would bring, and so pursued it whatever the cost. The readers are to follow that model.

scorning its shame. Crucifixion was considered so degrading that no Roman citizen could be crucified regardless of the crime committed.

Hebrews 12:3

Consider him. Instead of seeing opposition as an excuse to abandon faith, they should look to Jesus as a model of how to live faithfully through it.

weary and lose heart. These words were used in athletic circles to describe the collapse of a runner.

Hebrews 12:4

shedding your blood. The persecution they have experienced so far has not yet included the ultimate sacrifice made by Jesus.

Hebrews 12:7-11

A quote from Proverbs 3:11–12 (from the Septuagint), used to substantiate the author's point. At this time, corporal punishment of children was seen as a sign of a father's concern that his children learn right from wrong. Although children whose parents do not train or restrict them in any way seem to have more freedom, it is the children whose parents love them enough to administer discipline that grow into mature, responsible adults. In the same way, hardship is seen as a sign of God's care, since such discipline leads to growth in righteousness and peace.

7

NAVIGATING THE JOURNEY

 ʒet Ready

Spend a few moments getting to know God. Read one of these brief
passages each day, and be sure to write down anything He reveals to you.

MONDAY **Read Genesis 2:15**
What responsibilities do your parents give you? How do your present responsibilities differ from those you had as a small child?

TUESDAY **Read Genesis 2:16-17**
How much freedom do your parents allow you? Is it enough? How do you define "freedom"? Do you think you should have more?

WEDNESDAY **Read Genesis 3:1**
Do personal thoughts or other people ever cause you to doubt God's Word?

THURSDAY **Read Genesis 3:2-3**
How do you combat temptation? Do you find it easy to recall the commands of God? Why might someone choose not to trust in His promises?

FRIDAY   **Read Genesis 3:4**

What lie has the world fed you? What temptation most commonly captures your attention? Do you trust God's power to permanently remove that temptation from your life?

SATURDAY   **Read Genesis 3:5**

Are there times when you want to be like God? In what ways would it be impossible for you to be like Him? What problems might this pose?

SUNDAY   **Read Genesis 3:6**

How far would you go to get what you want? How many of your temptations are related to things you see? Do you think you would be tempted less if you didn't have the use of your eyes?

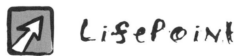

Knowing God and submitting to His authority in all things results in ultimate freedom.

SMALL-GROUP
TIME:
Divide into
smaller groups of
4-8, preferably in
a circle. You will
have a small-
group leader for
"Say What?"

 # Say What? *(15 MINUTES)*

Random Question of the Week:

What is a soufflé, and how do you make one?

Group Experience: Do You Trust Me?

1. How easy is it to trust someone?

2. What would a person have to do to earn your complete trust?

3. Does knowing a person increase or decrease your trust in him?

4. How might submitting to God result in freedom and trust?

LARGE-GROUP
TIME:
Turn to face
the front for this
teaching time.
Follow along and
take notes in your
Student Book.

So What? *(30 MINUTES)*

Who's in Charge?

1. Why might it be difficult to give your best when accountable to someone you dislike?

2. What might you be tempted to do when under the authority of many bosses?

Learning from the Bible Just in Case

[NARRATOR] ¹⁵ The Lᴏʀᴅ God took the man and placed him in the garden of Eden to work it and watch over it. ¹⁶ And the Lᴏʀᴅ God commanded the man,

[GOD] "You are free to eat from any tree of the garden, ¹⁷ but you must not eat from the tree of the knowledge of good and evil, for on the day you eat from it, you will certainly die."

[NARRATOR] ¹ Now the serpent was the most cunning of all the wild animals that the Lᴏʀᴅ God had made. He said to the woman,

[SERPENT] "Did God really say, 'You can't eat from any tree in the garden'?"

[NARRATOR] ² The woman said to the serpent,

[WOMAN] "We may eat the fruit from the trees in the garden. ³ But about the fruit of the tree in the middle of the garden, God said, 'You must not eat it or touch it, or you will die.'"

[SERPENT] ⁴ "No! You will not die,"

[NARRATOR] the serpent said to the woman.

[SERPENT] ⁵ "In fact, God knows that when you eat it your eyes will be opened and you will be like God, knowing good and evil."

[NARRATOR] ⁶ Then the woman saw that the tree was good for food and delightful to look at, and that it was desirable for obtaining wisdom. So she took some of its fruit and ate [it]; she also gave [some] to her husband, [who was] with her, and he ate [it].

Put God in Charge

3. God wants you to seek _____ first, placing His will _____ in your life.

4. _____ freedom comes from _____ to God's rule over your life.

5. Which of the following is most valuable to you?
   - ☐ My freedom
   - ☐ My future
   - ☐ My education
   - ☐ My friends

6. What is the difference between parental authority and God's authority?

7. For the Christ-follower, true maturity is seen in your _____ to place your life under God's _____, as you make _____ that coincide with His will and direction for your life.

8. How is living apart from God's authority like taking a train off its tracks?

God Rules

9. True or False: Adam and Eve could only stay in the garden if they followed a long list of rules.

10. When did Adam and Eve lose their freedom?

11. Why does God give us rules?

SMALL-GROUP
TIME:
Small-group
leaders will
direct your
discussions.
Everyone will
gain more if
you are open
and honest in
responding to
questions.

Do What? *(15 MINUTES)*

Group Experience: The Choice is Yours

1. Why do you think God made sure that Adam and Even knew the consequences of disobeying Him?
   - ☐ He wanted to protect them.
   - ☐ He wanted to show them how fair He is.
   - ☐ He wanted to prepare them for temptation.
   - ☐ He wanted them to appreciate their freedom.
   - ☐ He wanted them to understand sin.
   - ☐ Other: _____

2. What should you immediately do when tempted?
   - ☐ Ask your friends for advice.
   - ☐ Talk to your parents about it.
   - ☐ Ask God to give you the strength to resist.
   - ☐ Ask God for wisdom to know how to handle it.
   - ☐ Quote an appropriate Bible verse.
   - ☐ Ignore it.
   - ☐ Other: _____

3. To what authority figures do you have the most difficult time submitting? Why?

4. How willingly do you submit to God's authority? How might someone see that you are submissive to God's will?

Knowing God and submitting to His authority in all things results in ultimate freedom.

"DO" POINTS

These "Do" Points will help you grab hold of this week's LifePoint. Be open and honest as you answer the questions within your small group.

1. <u>List the positives and negatives of being under someone else's authority.</u> You will always be subject to someone. If not your parents, a teacher, coach, or boss. **What would be the worst thing that could happen to you if you totally submitted to God's authority?**

2. <u>List from Scripture the most difficult of God's commands to follow. Ask Him to give you the willingness to obey them.</u> God's Word is full of promises of love and forgiveness. It also contains some tough commands. **Which of God's commands is most difficult for you to obey? Why?**

3. <u>Daily spend time getting to better know God.</u> You spend time with the people you care about and enjoy being with. **How much time do you spend with God each day? What might that suggest about your relationship with Him? What does it say about your commitment?**

Prayer Connection:

This is the time to encourage, support, and pray for each other as you seek to better know God and submit to His authority.

Share prayer needs with the group, especially those related to submitting to God's authority and will. Your group facilitator will close your time in prayer.

Prayer Needs:

Remember your
"Get Ready" daily
Bible readings
and questions at
the beginning of
Session 8.

now What?

Take it to the next level by completing one of these assignments this week:

Option #1:

Write notes of appreciation to the adult authorities that God has placed in your life. Thank your teacher, coach, or boss for investing in you. Express appreciation for the things you are learning under their influence. Consider writing a similar note to your parents. (You'll give them a wonderful shock!)

Option #2:

Plan to spend time with the Lord each day. Use the time to talk to God through prayer, and learn about His plans for your life through reading Scripture and meditating on it. Ask another person to help keep you accountable. Specifically ask God to help you submit to His authority and to the others He has placed in your life.

Bible Reference Notes

Use these notes to deepen your understanding as you study the Bible on your own:

Genesis 2:15

work ... take care. Work was part of God's plan from the beginning. Man was given the responsibility of being an obedient servant and wise steward.

Genesis 2:16

any tree. God gave Adam the freedom to choose which tree he would eat from. This included the tree of life mentioned in Genesis 2:9.

Genesis 2:17

tree of the knowledge of good and evil. This tree was placed in the garden to give Adam and Eve the opportunity to exercise their freedom of choice. Every tree was appealing, but only one was off limits. This "tree" gave them the opportunity to express their obedience and trust in God. The presence of evil was not in the substance of the fruit itself. They sinned in their attempt to gain God's knowledge independently of Him.

surely die. Disobeying God results in spiritual death and ultimately physical death. The eating of the forbidden fruit in itself would not result in death. The act of disobedience to God that prompted taking the fruit brought death.

Genesis 3:1

the serpent. While Satan is not referred to in this story, Revelation 12:9 and 20:2 identify Satan with the serpent.

Genesis 3:3

the tree that is in the middle of the garden. This was the tree of the knowledge of good and evil (Gen. 2:9,17). Popular depictions show it as an apple tree, but Scripture does not identify it with any known fruit. Why was the tree there if God did not want them to eat of it? Perhaps because God wanted people to have a choice about whether to obey Him or not.

or you will die. The clear implication is that God did not originally intend people to have to experience even physical death. Physical death came as a result of human sin (see Rom. 5:12–14).

Genesis 3:5

you will be like God. This is the basis of much of the temptation we face—that we try to be like God. Specific situations in the Bible where this was the case include the Tower of Babel (Gen. 11:1–9), God's answer to Job (Job 40:6–41:34), and Christ's third temptation (Matt. 4:8–9). And a prime example is Lucifer's (Satan's) rebellion in heaven that caused him to be cast out of God's presence (Isa. 14:12–15).

NOTES

Session
8

SOLVING THE MAZE

Get Ready

Spend a few moments getting to know God. Read one of these brief passages each day, and be sure to write down anything He reveals to you.

MONDAY

Read Psalm 19:7-8

What practical benefits have you experienced from knowing the promises of Scripture? How does knowing God's Word change the way you look at the world?

TUESDAY

Read Psalm 19:9-10

How does your daily routine indicate the value you place on the Bible? Could you honestly say that you love God's Word? If so, how do you show it?

WEDNESDAY

Read Psalm 19:11

Have you ever read something in the Bible that helped you through hardship? What are some rewards of following God's instructions?

THURSDAY   Read James 1:22

What does it take to move you to action? Have you ever been deceived? Think about the impact of being deceived had on you. How did it make you feel?

FRIDAY   Read James 1:23

Who do you see when you look in the mirror? Are you content to hear God's commands without changing your life or personally getting involved in ministry?

SATURDAY   Read James 1:24

Can you remember the last compliment you received? What do you think people would say is the best thing about you? Are you a person of your word or God's Word?

SUNDAY   Read James 1:25

Is it painful to take an honest look at yourself? When you look closely at yourself, what do you see? How likely are you to do whatever it takes to be more like God?

 LifePoint

Regularly reading and studying the Bible reveals promises, principles, and truths for making critical decisions.

SMALL-GROUP
TIME:
Divide into
smaller groups of
4-8, preferably in
a circle. You will
have a small-
group leader for
"Say What?"

Say What? *(15 MINUTES)*

Random Question of the Week:
If you could live on another planet, which would you choose?

Group Experience: What Time Is It?
1. How do you spend most of your time each day?

2. Did the ticking clock help to focus or distract you?

3. How do your drawings represent the decisions you make regarding how you spend your time?

4. How does the time you spend reading and studying your Bible compare with the time you spend on other activities? What, if anything, will you do about it?

So What? *(30 MINUTES)*

Learn the Rules

1. Why isn't the Bible lived out in the lives of more people?

Learning from the Bible ...

James 1:22-25

Learning from the Bible

22 But be doers of the word and not hearers only, deceiving yourselves. 23 Because if anyone is a hearer of the word and not a doer, he is like a man looking at his own face in a mirror; 24 for he looks at himself, goes away, and right away forgets what kind of man he was. 25 But the one who looks intently into the perfect law of freedom and perseveres in it, and is not a forgetful hearer but a doer who acts—this person will be blessed in what he does.

Just Do It

2. List three advantages to reading and studying God's Word.

    1.

    2.

    3.

Three Ways to Get the Maximum Benefit from God's Word

3. In order to experience the full benefit of Scripture you must ...

☐ Read, reread, and listen to it.

☐ Analyze, ponder, and pick it apart.

☐ Study, memorize, and apply it to your life.

A Three-Step Process for Applying God's Word

4. List the three steps to applying Scripture.

1.

2.

3.

 Do What? *(15 MINUTES)*

Group Experience: Grasping God's Word

You will participate in an activity led by your small-group leader.

8

Regularly reading and studying the Bible reveals promises, principles, and truths for making critical decisions.

These "Do" Points will help you grab hold of this week's LifePoint. Be open and honest as you answer the questions within your small group.

1. Worship service is only one place where you can hear the Word of God. Other places may include Bible study or a small accountability group. You may also hear the Word of God through some music.
   How might taking notes on worship and Bible reading benefit you?

2. Make a plan to regularly read and study Scripture. The Bible is full of poetry, history, adventure, bravery, and so much more! Best of all, it offers guidelines for living.
   Can you make a commitment to read the Bible every day? If so, what's your action plan?

3. Keep a journal of what you are learning from the Bible. Journaling is a great way to better understand what you are reading. It can help you make connections between the words of Scripture and the things going on in your life.
   Have you ever kept a personal diary at home or a journal for a class? Will you begin one to record what God is telling you through His Word?

Prayer Connection:

This is the time to encourage, support, and pray for each other as you read and study the Bible to discover tools for godly living.

Share prayer needs with the group, especially those related to personal Bible study. Your group facilitator will close your time in prayer.

Prayer Needs:

Remember your "Get Ready" daily Bible readings and questions at the beginning of Session 9.

now What?

Take it to the next level by completing one of these assignments this week:

Option #1:
Consider the "Do What?" activity, "Grasping God's Word." Research the Bible to find out more about the six disciplines to better understanding Scripture. Hint: Psalm 119:11 can be used to support one of them. Trace the outline of your hand on a sheet of paper, and label your fingers and palm with the corresponding Scripture references.

Option #2:
Create your own sermon-notes notebook. Fill a small binder with paper, and begin taking notes on each Sunday's sermon. At the top of each page, list the date, the name of the person preaching, the topic, and the Scripture references cited. As you listen to God's Word being preached, take notes.

Bible Reference notes

Use these notes to deepen your understanding as you study the Bible on your own:

James 1:22

merely listen. The Christian must not just hear the Word of God. A response is required.
deceive yourselves. To make mere knowledge of God's will the sole criterion for the religious life is dangerous and self-deceptive.
Do what it says. This is James' main point in this section.

James 1:23-24

James illustrates his point with a metaphor. The person who reads Scripture (which is a mirror to the Christian, because in it his or her true state is shown), and then goes away unchanged is like the person who gets up in the morning and sees how dirty and disheveled he or she is, but then promptly forgets about it (when the proper response would be to get cleaned up).

James 1:25

the perfect law. The reference is probably to the teachings of Jesus that set one free, in contrast to the Jewish law, which brought bondage (see Rom. 8:2).
continues. Such people make obedience to the gospel a continuing part of their lives.
blessed. The sheer act of keeping this law is a happy experience in and of itself because it produces good fruit, now and in the future.

NOTES

NOTES

9

REFLECTING CHRIST THROUGH THE JOURNEY

 Get Ready

Spend a few moments getting to know God. Read one of these brief passages each day, and be sure to write down anything He reveals to you.

MONDAY   **Read John 16:5-6**
What is your first reaction when a trusted and good friend is removed from your life? Do you feel abandoned? Do you question God? If you were able to see every-thing—past, present, and future—at once, how would it change the way you feel?

TUESDAY   **Read John 16:7-8**
Would you be willing to give up the best thing you've ever had for the promise of something even better? Think about what might be better than "the best thing you've ever had." How easily would you put faith in that kind of promise?

9

WEDNESDAY   **Read John 16:9**
Do you understand "sin" as a list of things in your life, or an alien force that co-exists with who you really are? What is the difference? What does the difference mean to you right now?

THURSDAY   **Read John 16:10**

Would you have liked to personally know Jesus when He walked the earth? If you had been His friend during that time, do you think doing the right thing would have been easier or more difficult than it is now? Why?

FRIDAY   **Read John 16:11**

Are you judgmental? Is it ever all right to pass judgment on something evil? By what standard do you judge right and wrong?

SATURDAY   **Read John 16:12-13**

When is enough, enough? Is it possible for anything to be too good? Can you handle the truth? Ask God what it means to be guided into "all truth."

SUNDAY   **Read John 16:14-16**

What do you consider the most reliable method of delivering a message? Would you trust a singing telegram? What is the best news you've ever received?

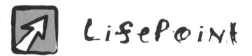

Guiding the believer to live in such a way as to reflect Christ in all areas, the Holy Spirit is God's personal presence with us.

SMALL-GROUP
TIME:
Divide into
smaller groups of
4-8, preferably in
a circle. You will
have a small-
group leader for
"Say What?"

Say What? *(15 MINUTES)*

Random Question of the Week:
What makes tomatoes fruits instead of vegetables?

Group Experience: Blind Simon Says
1. How did the blindfold affect the way you played the game?

2. Were you more concerned about yourself or the other players?

3. How do you know that everyone was playing fair?

4. How do you know that you were not the only one blindfolded?

5. How is playing "Blind Simon Says" like following the Holy Spirit's direction in your life?

9

LARGE-GROUP TIME:
Turn to face the front for this teaching time. Follow along and take notes in your *Student Book.*

So What? *(30 MINUTES)*

The Voices You Hear

1. What are three of the Holy Spirit's functions?

   1.

   2.

   3.

2. What has the Lord called you to do?

Learning from the Bible

Learning from the Bible ...

John 16:5-16

[5] "But now I am going away to Him who sent Me, and not one of you asks Me, 'Where are You going?' [6] Yet, because I have spoken these things to you, sorrow has filled your heart. [7] Nevertheless, I am telling you the truth. It is for your benefit that I go away, because if I don't go away the Counselor will not come to you. If I go, I will send Him to you. [8] When He comes, He will convict the world about sin, righteousness, and judgment: [9] about sin, because they do not believe in Me; [10] about righteousness, because I am going to the Father and you will no longer see Me; [11] and about judgment, because the ruler of this world has been judged.

[12] "I still have many things to tell you, but you can't bear them now. [13] When the Spirit of truth comes, He will guide you into all the truth. For He will not speak on His own, but He will speak whatever He hears. He will also declare to you what is to come. [14] He will glorify Me, because He will take from what is Mine and declare it to you. [15] Everything the Father has is Mine. This is why I told you that He takes from what is Mine and will declare it to you.

[16] "A little while and you will no longer see Me; again a little while and you will see Me."

The Holy Spirit's Role in the World

3. List three functions of the Holy Spirit.

   1.

   2.

   3.

The Holy Spirit's Personal Presence in Your Life

4. In the same way Jesus _____ and _____ the disciples, the
   _____ continues to teach and guide those who _____
   Christ.

5. On whose authority does the Holy Spirit speak?

   ☐ God's

   ☐ Yours

   ☐ Nobody knows

6. True or False: The Holy Spirit uses Scripture, godly counsel, and prayer to
   communicate to you.

9

7. How can you sense the Holy Spirit's guidance?

SMALL-GROUP
TIME:
Small-group
leaders will
direct your
discussions.
Today you
will focus on
connecting with
your heart and
connecting
with God.

 # Do What? *(15 MINUTES)*

Group Experience: Too Much Noise

1. Name some of the good noises in the world. Then list some of the bad.

2. The world is full of so much noise that it is sometimes difficult to hear God's voice. What do you need to do in order to hear God?

   ☐ Turn your music down

   ☐ Read the Bible more

   ☐ Stop watching TV

   ☐ Spend less time with friends

   ☐ Memorize Scripture

   ☐ Play video games less

   ☐ Wake up earlier and spend some quiet time with God

   ☐ Spend the last minutes of your day with God

   ☐ Pray more often

3. Jesus says, "My sheep hear my voice, I know them, and they follow Me" (John 10:27). How have you most recently been aware of Jesus' voice? What did you feel His Spirit prompting you to do?

Guiding the believer to live in such a way as to reflect Christ in all areas, the Holy Spirit is God's personal presence with us.

These "Do" Points will help you grab hold of this week's LifePoint. Be open and honest as you answer the questions within your small group.

1. Listen for the Spirit's promptings. God speaks to you through your conscience and the peace—or lack of it— that you feel.
   What is the Holy Spirit telling you to do?

2. Keep a journal of the Holy Spirit's activity in your life. Whether you realize it or not, God is always working in and around you.
   Are you able to easily identify the Holy Spirit's work in your life? How can you tell if God is working in you or if you're trying to do things in your own power?

3. Pray that God will give you peace in making decisions. Every day you are forced to make decisions. Some are easy. Others require prayerful consideration.
   What decision faces you that requires God's help? How likely are you to follow His counsel?

Prayer Connection:

This is the time to encourage, support, and pray for each other as you trust the Holy Spirit to guide you in how to live for Christ.

Share prayer needs with the group, especially those related to seeking the Holy Spirit's guidance in your life. Your group facilitator will close your time in prayer.

Prayer Needs:

Remember your
"Get Ready" daily
Bible readings
and questions at
the beginning of
Session 10.

now What?

Take it to the next level by completing one of these assignments this week:

Option #1:

Spend 15 minutes each day reading your Bible in a quiet place. Begin your time with a simple prayer, asking God to open your heart and mind to His Will. Do not ask for anything else. As you spend time meditating on Scripture, keep a journal nearby. As the Holy Spirit prompts you, record what He brings to mind.

Option #2:

List three decisions you face this week. Keep the list in your Bible and refer to it at least twice a day. Every time you read it, pray that the Holy Spirit will guide you to do the make the right decisions—decisions that honor God.

Bible Reference Notes

Use these notes to deepen your understanding as you study the Bible on your own:

John 16:5

none of you asks. Peter did ask this question in John 13:36: "Lord, where are you going?" and Jesus replied: "Where I am going, you cannot follow now, but you will follow later." Some commentators see this as evidence that chapters 13–16 are a compilation of several teachings of Jesus arranged in this format to give a summary of Jesus' teaching to believers. Others think that Jesus is responding to the fact that Peter didn't understand the significance of the answer Jesus gave to Peter's question.

John 16:7

It is for your good that I am going away. Jesus' departure meant the coming of the Counselor. The Greek term used for the Holy Spirit is *paraclete*. It is a rich term for which there is no adequate English translation. Attempts such as Counselor or Helper or Comforter fail because they emphasize only one of many aspects of the term. Jesus is telling the disciples that He will return to them in a deep, inner, spiritual way. He had also referred to the Spirit in John 7:38–39: "Whoever believes in me, as the Scripture has said, streams of living water will flow from within him." By this He meant the Spirit, whom those who believed in Him were later to receive. Up to that time the Spirit had not been given, since Jesus had not yet been glorified (see also John 14:15–18).

John 16:8

he will convict the world of guilt in regard to sin and righteousness and judgment. The "world" held that Jesus was an unrighteous sinner under the judgment of God (John 9:24). The Spirit will prove that the world is wrong about its convictions on these matters. "Righteousness" (perhaps better translated as "justice") is shown by the Father's vindication of Jesus through His resurrection and ascension (v. 10).

John 16:13

He will not speak on his own. Jesus only speaks the words of His Father; the Spirit only speaks the words of Jesus. Each member of the Trinity seeks the glory and honor of the other (see John 8:54; 12:28; 16:14; 17:1,4–5).

John 16:15

All that belongs to the Father is mine ... the Spirit will ... make it known to you. The incredible truth of the gospel is that God has fully revealed Himself to His people. Even believers who never saw Jesus physically are not at a disadvantage compared to those who did, for the Spirit continually reveals Jesus and the Father to whomever comes in faith to Christ.

John 16:16

In a little while ... then after a little while. This riddle may be intentionally ambiguous. Does the first "little while" mean after His resurrection or after His return in glory? Does "seeing" mean physical sight or spiritual sight—as it so often does in this Gospel? If the latter, then the second "little while" may mean His coming to them by His Spirit (John 14:18–20). It would not be unlike this author to mean all the above!

NOTES

OBSTACLES ALONG THE WAY

 Get Ready

*Spend a few moments getting to know God. Read one of these brief
passages each day, and be sure to write down anything He reveals to you.*

MONDAY

Read Genesis 45:4-5

Have you ever looked into the eyes of someone you intentionally hurt? What did you
expect that person to say or do? Were you surprised by their words or actions?

TUESDAY

Read Genesis 45:6-11

Who, in addition to your parents, has God placed in your life to take care of you?
How does God speak to you through the care provided?

WEDNESDAY

Read Genesis 50:15

In what do you place your sense of security? If that possession, principle, or person
were taken away from you, how would it change your outlook on life?

THURSDAY

Read Genesis 50:16-17

What is the worst thing you've ever experienced? How long did it take you to over-
come it? Had you forgotten about it until now?

FRIDAY **Read Genesis 50:18-19**

Is there a person in your life that deserves your mercy? Think of ways that you can show mercy to those around you. Why would you decide to do this?

SATURDAY **Read Genesis 50:20**

What have you done that turned out exactly the opposite from what you expected? List ways that God can make all things work for the good of those who seek to follow His ways.

SUNDAY **Read Genesis 50:21**

When have your words delivered comfort to someone in need? How has someone else's kindness calmed your fears?

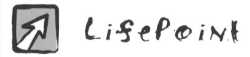 LifePoint

God uses everything we experience—even the most difficult circumstances—to accomplish His will and form our character for navigating the critical path.

SMALL-GROUP
TIME:
Divide into
smaller groups of
4-8, preferably in
a circle. You will
have a small-
group leader for
"Say What?"

 # Say What? *(15 MINUTES)*

Random Question of the Week:
What is your favorite gadget?

Group Experience: Worst Case Scenario
1. If this described your day, what would have been the worst part?

2. At what point would you have given up?

3. How could God use a day like this to accomplish His will and mature our faith in Him?

LARGE-GROUP
TIME:
Turn to face
the front for this
teaching time.
Follow along and
take notes in your
Student Book.

So What? *(30 MINUTES)*

10

Bad Things Happen
1. Your _____ to the circumstances in your life will determine your level of _____ in making _____ _____ along the way.

2. What was key to Job's experiencing great blessings after such tragedy?

Learning from the Bible

[NARRATOR] *4 Then Joseph said to his brothers,*

[JOSEPH] "Please, come near me,"

[NARRATOR] and they came near.

[JOSEPH] "I am Joseph, your brother,"

[NARRATOR] he said,

[JOSEPH] "the one you sold into Egypt. 5 And now don't be worried or angry with your-selves for selling me here, because God sent me ahead of you to preserve life. 6 For the famine has been in the land these two years, and there will be five more years without plowing or harvesting. 7 God sent me ahead of you to establish you as a remnant within the land and to keep you alive by a great deliverance. 8 Therefore it was not you who sent me here, but God. He has made me a father to Pharaoh, lord of his entire household, and ruler over all the land of Egypt.

9 "Return quickly to my father and say to him, 'This is what your son Joseph says: "God has made me lord of all Egypt. Come down to me without delay. 10 You can settle in the land of Goshen and be near me—you, your children, and grandchildren, your sheep, cattle, and all you have. 11 There I will sustain you, for there will be five more years of famine. Otherwise, you, your household, and everything you have will become destitute." '

[NARRATOR] 15 When Joseph's brothers saw that their father was dead, they said to one another,

[BROTHERS] "If Joseph is holding a grudge against us, he will certainly repay us for all the wrong we caused him."

[NARRATOR] 16 So they sent this message to Joseph,

[BROTHERS] "Before he died your father gave a command: 17 'Say this to Joseph: Please forgive your brothers' transgression and their sin—the wrong they caused you.' Therefore, please forgive the transgression of the servants of the God of your father."

[NARRATOR] Joseph wept when their message came to him. 18 Then his brothers also came to him, bowed down before him, and said,

[BROTHERS] "We are your slaves!"

[NARRATOR] [19] But Joseph said to them,

[JOSEPH]"Don't be afraid. Am I in the place of God? [20] You planned evil against me; God planned it for good to bring about the present result—the survival of many people. [21] Therefore don't be afraid. I will take care of you and your little ones."

[NARRATOR] And he comforted them and spoke kindly to them.

Responding to Difficult Circumstances

3. What are the two ways you can choose to respond to adversity?

   1.

   2.

4. Give three ways God can use the circumstances in your life.

   1.

   2.

   3.

5. Check the methods God may use to get your attention:

   ☐ Through something your parents say
   ☐ Through the way He answers your prayers
   ☐ Through the amount of time He takes to answer your prayers
   ☐ Through hurt feelings
   ☐ Through sickness
   ☐ Through blessings
   ☐ Through tragedy
   ☐ Through good friendships
   ☐ Through bad friendships

Honoring God in All Circumstances

6. In what three ways did Joseph deal with his circumstances?

   1.

   2.

   3.

10

SMALL-GROUP
TIME:
Small-group
leaders will
direct your
discussions.
Everyone will
gain more if
you are open
and honest in
responding to
questions.

Do What? *(15 MINUTES)*

Group Experience: Lessons from the Pit

1. If you were Joseph, what would you have done to your brothers when they came to you for help?
   - ☐ Forgive them
   - ☐ Throw them in a pit
   - ☐ Make them serve you as your slaves
   - ☐ Have them killed
   - ☐ Make them sweat, and then forgive them
   - ☐ Nothing
   - ☐ Feed them and send them on their way
   - ☐ Other: _____

2. Describe a "pit" in your life that you've recently faced. How was your perspective different when you looked up from the pit? What did that situation teach you?

3. In what area do you have the most trouble when facing tough times?
   - ☐ Blaming others
   - ☐ Becoming bitter
   - ☐ Questioning God's timing

4. What do you need to do in order to honor God in that area?

God uses everything we experience—even the most difficult circumstances—to accomplish His will and form our character for navigating the critical path.

These "Do" Points will help you grab hold of this week's LifePoint. Be open and honest as you answer the questions within your small group.

1. Spend time with Christians whose faith has matured through adversity. Many people can minister to you by sharing how God has worked in their lives. **Share your struggles with someone who truly cares about you and can help.**

2. Study biblical accounts of people who experienced great adversity and discovered God's will for their lives. Both the Old and New Testaments are full of the stories of men and women who suffered hardship and yet still honored God. **What can you learn from these heroes of the faith?**

3. Confess to God any bitterness that has resulted from trials you've experienced. If you can't be honest with God, you can't be honest with anyone. God knows all your thoughts, good and bad. **How can you be more honest in your conversations with God?**

Prayer Connection:

This is the time to encourage, support, and pray for each other for God's help and encouragement through difficult circumstances.

Share prayer needs with the group, especially those related to difficult circumstances you face or soon will. Your group facilitator will close your time in prayer.

10

Prayer Needs:

Remember your
"Get Ready" daily
Bible readings
and questions at
the beginning of
Session 11.

now What?

Take it to the next level by completing one of these assignments this week:

Option #1:

Adopt the role of a reporter and get the scoop. Write an article as if you're reporting on an event in the life of a person from Scripture who experienced terrible circumstances, yet honored God. Consider Moses, Ruth, David, Paul, Mary, and Jesus. Or you could grab a friend and do a mock interview with one of these individuals. Record his or her character traits, the circumstances he or she experienced, and how God used the circumstances to bring about good.

Option #2:

Tape a conversation with a mature Christian who has experienced terrible hardships yet believes God used those difficulties for a specific reason. After you tape the person's story, listen again to what was said. Pray that God will develop the character traits and faith the person shows in your own life.

Bible Reference Notes

Use these notes to deepen your understanding as you study the Bible on your own:

Genesis 45:4   *I am your brother Joseph.* Joseph's brothers were terrified of their brother whom they had sold into slavery (see Gen. 37:28). Joseph had the power to exact revenge on them because of their betrayal if he chose to do so.

Genesis 45:5   *God sent me.* God was working behind the scenes to carry out His purposes, namely to preserve the nation of Israel during the famine. God used Joseph as His chosen instrument in the palace of the pharaoh. God would not allow the evil actions of people to dictate his plan. Instead, we see God's sovereign control in human affairs.

Genesis 45:7   *a remnant.* God would not allow His chosen people, Israel, to die because of the famine.

Genesis 45:8   *father.* This was a title of honor given to high officials in Egypt.
lord ... ruler. Joseph's power was almost absolute; in Egypt, he was second only to pharaoh.

Genesis 50:17   *Joseph wept.* Joseph was both emotional and sensitive (see Gen. 42:24; 43:30; 45:2,14–15; 46:29).

Genesis 50:18   *threw themselves down.* This was a fulfillment of Joseph's earlier dreams (see Gen. 37:7,9).

Genesis 50:19   *Am I in the place of God?* Joseph wanted his brothers to know that he wasn't interested in playing God by seeking revenge on them. Joseph knew that God was the only One who could deal with injustices.

Genesis 50:20   God used the evil treatment of Joseph's brothers, being falsely accused by Potiphar's wife, and being forgotten in prison, to achieve His purpose. When we trust God during difficult times, He is faithful to work good from it.
God intended it for good. On the surface, what Joseph's brothers did to him was a terrible act. Behind the scenes, however, God was making sure Joseph was in the right position to carry out His greater plan—to save the lives of the people of Israel and the other nations who came to buy food during the famine.

NOTES

11

LEANING ON OTHERS IN THE STORY

 Get Ready

Spend a few moments getting to know God. Read one of these brief passages each day, and be sure to write down anything He reveals to you.

MONDAY

Read 1 Kings 12:1-4

When did you last make an agreement with someone that included a condition? What made you decide to bargain with that person?

TUESDAY

Read 1 Kings 12:5

If you knew an answer would change your life, how long would you be willing to wait for it? Could you wait three whole days?

WEDNESDAY

Read 1 Kings 12:6-11

From whom do you most often seek advice? Are you more likely to follow the advice of an older adult or that of a peer?

11

THURSDAY

Read 1 Kings 12:12-14

Describe a time when you totally disagreed with advice you received. Did you follow it, or did you make a different decision on your own?

FRIDAY   **Read Proverbs 15:22**

Which of your plans have succeeded? Which have failed? What role has godly counsel played in your planning?

SATURDAY   **Read Proverbs 3:7**

What if you were the only person to turn to for help? Would you trust your own counsel, or would you become even more dependent on God's wisdom?

SUNDAY   **Read Proverbs 12:15**

How often are your decisions correct? How often do you admit, at least to yourself, that you are wrong? What is the most foolish thing you ever decided to do?

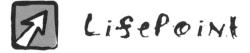 LifePoint

God places specific Christians in our lives so that we may be formed spiritually in a way that allows us to become the men and women God created us to be.

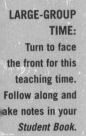

SMALL-GROUP
TIME:
Divide into
smaller groups of
4-8, preferably in
a circle. You will
have a small-
group leader for
"Say What?"

Say What? *(15 MINUTES)*

Random Question of the Week:
What is your favorite breakfast cereal?

Group Experience: Whom Would You Trust?
1. In each case, why did you choose the person you chose?

2. In what situations could you benefit from having more than one person to go to for help?

3. To whom can go for godly advice? Have you ever sought someone out for this reason?

LARGE-GROUP
TIME:
Turn to face
the front for this
teaching time.
Follow along and
take notes in your
Student Book.

So What? *(30 MINUTES)*

Everybody Needs a Little Help Sometimes
1. True or False: There is shame in asking for assistance.

2. How do people look for advice?

Learning from the Bible

1 Then Rehoboam went to Shechem, for all Israel had gone to Shechem to make him king. 2 When Jeroboam son of Nebat heard [about it], for he was still in Egypt where he had fled from King Solomon's presence, Jeroboam stayed in Egypt. 3 They summoned him, and Jeroboam and the whole assembly of Israel came and spoke to Rehoboam: 4 "Your father made our yoke harsh. You, therefore, lighten your father's harsh service and the heavy yoke he put on us, and we will serve you."

11

5 Rehoboam replied, "Go home for three days and then return to me." So the people left. 6 Then King Rehoboam consulted with the elders who had served his father Solomon when he was alive, asking, "How do you advise me to respond to these people?"

7 They replied, "Today if you will be a servant to these people and serve them, and if you respond to them by speaking kind words to them, they will be your servants forever."

8 But he rejected the advice of the elders who had advised him and consulted with the young men who had grown up with him and served him. 9 He asked them, "What message do you advise that we send back to these people who said to me, 'Lighten the yoke your father put on us'?"

10 Then the young men who had grown up with him told him, "This is what you should say to these people who said to you, 'Your father made our yoke heavy, but you, make it lighter on us!' This is what you should tell them: 'My little finger is thicker than my father's loins! 11 Although my father burdened you with a heavy yoke, I will add to your yoke; my father disciplined you with whips, but I will discipline you with barbed whips.' "

12 So Jeroboam and all the people came to Rehoboam on the third day, as the king had ordered: "Return to me on the third day." 13 Then the king answered the people harshly. He rejected the advice the elders had given him 14 and spoke to them according to the young men's advice: "My father made your yoke heavy, but I will add to your yoke; my father disciplined you with whips, but I will discipline you with barbed whips."

Some People Intentionally Don't Seek Counsel
3. For some people, making decisions causes ...
   - ☐ Hives
   - ☐ An adrenaline rush
   - ☐ Stress

4. For what three reasons might you not seek godly advice?
   1.
   2.
   3.

5. Seeking godly counsel is a good idea for two reasons. (1) Sometimes you can only see things the way _____ want to see them, and (2) sometimes you don't have enough _____ to make the right decision on your own.

Characteristics of Godly Counsel

6. Check the statements that describe ways to choose wise advisors:

☐ Choose your best friend

☐ Pick someone who tells you what you want to hear

☐ Pick someone who tells you the truth no matter what you want to hear

☐ Choose an adviser who is where you want to be in life

☐ Find the oldest person in the world

☐ Choose more than one person to be your counselor

☐ Choose one person to be your counselor and stick with them

7. Often the best advice comes from the combined wisdom of several ...

☐ People

☐ Friends

☐ Children

☐ Theologians

8. Be sure to _____ the right _____ when seeking godly counsel.

9. What two questions should you ask a counselor?

1.

2.

10. True or False: You can take everything a Christian counselor tells you as God's personal word to you.

SMALL-GROUP
TIME:
Small-group
leaders will
direct your
discussions.
Everyone will
gain more if
you are open
and honest in
responding to
questions.

 Do What? *(15 MINUTES)*

Group Experience: The Cost of Godly Counsel

1. What advice would you have given Rehoboam? Would you have sided with the young guys, the old men, or offered your own counsel regarding the situation?

2. In order to receive godly counsel you can depend on, what would you be willing to give?

☐ An hour a week
☐ Fifteen minutes every day
☐ My pride
☐ One weekend a year
☐ $100
☐ As much time as it takes
☐ Other: _____

3. In each of the following areas, write one sentence describing advice you've been given:

Friendships

Time management

Dealing with disappointment

Family problems

Study habits

Being the best

4. What is the godliest counsel that you have received? Who or what was its source?

LIFEPOINT REVIEW

God places specific Christians in our lives so that we may be formed spiritually in a way that allows us to become the men and women God created us to be.

"DO" POINTS

These "Do" Points will help you grab hold of this week's LifePoint. Be open and honest as you answer the questions within your small group.

1. Compile a list of people to whom you can go for godly advice. There is more than one person who can help you find godly answers.
   Who will you be on your list of godly counselors?

2. Ask the right questions from godly counsel. Getting counsel requires more than just "sitting and soaking." You need to ask questions and respond to what you hear.
   Do you talk too much in a conversation? Too little? What can you do to be more responsive in a counseling situation?

3. <u>Listen for God's voice through the counsel of others.</u> God does speak through those who serve Him. He uses His Word and His Spirit to validate the words spoken on His behalf.
   Will you prayerfully consider the advice you receive?

Prayer Connection:

This is the time to encourage, support, and pray for each other as you realize that God has placed people in your lives who can provide wise counsel.

Share prayer needs with the group, especially those related to finding the right people counselors. Your group facilitator will close your time in prayer.

Prayer Needs:

Remember your "Get Ready" daily Bible readings and questions at the beginning of Session 12.

Take it to the next level by completing one of these assignments this week:

Option #1:
Proverbs is a book of wisdom; try to read a chapter a day. A neat thing about the book is that there's a proverb for every day of the month. This week, begin reading the chapter that matches the calendar day. For example, if you begin reading on the sixteenth of the month, then begin with Proverbs 16. Read chapter 17 the following day. Consider reading the book Proverbs every month throughout the year.

Option #2:
Contact three mature Christian adults from whom you would consider seeking counsel. Ask them if they would consider being a person that you can go to when you need godly advice. Set up a time to meet with each of them, and pray with them that God would use them to help you find His direction.

11

Bible Reference Notes

Use these notes to deepen your understanding as you study the Bible on your own:

1 Kings 12:1

Shechem. Located about 35 miles north of Jerusalem. This was a significant city in Israel's history. For example, this is where the Israelites dedicated themselves to keeping the Mosaic Law (Josh. 24:1–27). After Israel divided into two kingdoms, Shechem became the capital of the northern kingdom for a short period (1 Kings 12:25).

1 Kings 12:2-5

Israel wanted Jeroboam to convey their concerns over labor and taxation before Rehoboam. The prophet Ahijah had already told Jeroboam that he would eventually rule 10 of the tribes after the kingdom divided. Jeroboam apparently didn't try to press the issue but, instead, let events play out naturally.

1 Kings 12:6

the elders. Rehoboam sought input from those who had served as his father's official advisers. These elders were most likely the same age as Solomon.

1 Kings 12:7

If today you will be a servant. Great leaders in God's economy are those who have a servant's heart like Jesus'.

1 Kings 12:8

young men. Rehoboam assembled some of his own friends and associates for advice. Apparently, they were already serving him in some official capacity.

1 Kings 12:10

My little finger is thicker than my father's waist. This hyperbole meant that the least severe treatment by Rehoboam would be far greater than his father's most oppressive measures.

1 Kings 12:11

scorpions. These were leather lashes with sharp pieces of metal attached to them; it was a cruel whip used during this time.

1 Kings 12:12-14

Rather than listening to the elders' advice, Rehoboam decided to serve his own interests and actually increase the burden on the people. This decision would contribute to the eventual division of the kingdom.

THROUGH THE LABRYRINTH OF LIFE

 Get Ready

Spend a few moments getting to know God. Read one of these brief passages each day, and be sure to write down anything He reveals to you.

MONDAY

Read James 1:1-2

How does it make you feel when someone tells you to look on the bright side? Does anyone have the right to tell you how you should feel?

TUESDAY

Read James 1:3-4

What is the first thing you do in a desperate situation? How much do you try to endure before asking God for help?

WEDNESDAY

Read James 1:5

What is the last thing you asked God for? Do you think you have wisdom, or do you feel you lack it? Why would anyone not ask God for wisdom?

THURSDAY

Read James 1:6

When you ask God for something, do you really believe He will give you what's best for you? Are you ever indecisive? When you're caught between two choices, and struggle to have confidence that God will reveal Himself to you, how do you feel? What does this say about what you really believe?

12

FRIDAY **Read James 1:7-8**

How long does it take you to make a decision? What might cause you to fear making a decision?

SATURDAY **Read James 1:9-11**

How does a delicate flower respond to the scorching summer heat? How can this be applied to our lives and the lives of others? Think about the ways you can protect yourself from the scorching heat of life?

SUNDAY **Read James 1:12**

Describe a spiritual struggle you have endured. How did you feel God's hand during the struggle? In what ways did this struggle contribute to a greater understanding?

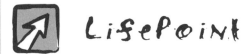 LifePoint

Making the critical decisions amidst life's adversities requires a wisdom unavailable by any means other than God.

SMALL-GROUP
TIME:
Divide into
smaller groups of
4-8, preferably in
a circle. You will
have a small-
group leader for
"Say What?"

Say What? *(15 MINUTES)*

Random Question of the Week:

Why do people refer to some shoes as tennis shoes even though they are not made for tennis and are rarely used for tennis?

Group Experience: Truth and Consequence

1. Did you identify every false statment? If not, how many did you get?

2. What method did you use to determine the three true statements from the false one?

3. On what do you rely on or trust?

4. How, in the challenging times of your life, is your reliance on God and trust in His wisdom evident?

LARGE-GROUP
TIME:
Turn to face
the front for this
teaching time.
Follow along and
take notes in your
Student Book.

So What? *(30 MINUTES)*

It's Just the Way It Is

1. There are times when you will not know what _____ you should make or how to _____ when the going gets tough.

2. What was God's response to Solomon's request for wisdom?

12

Learning from the Bible

[1] James, a slave of God and of the Lord Jesus Christ:
To the 12 tribes in the Dispersion.
Greetings.

[2] Consider it a great joy, my brothers, whenever you experience various trials, [3] knowing that the testing of your faith produces endurance. [4] But endurance must do its complete work, so that you may be mature and complete, lacking nothing.

[5] Now if any of you lacks wisdom, he should ask God, who gives to all generously and without criticizing, and it will be given to him. [6] But let him ask in faith without doubting. For the doubter is like the surging sea, driven and tossed by the wind. [7] That person should not expect to receive anything from the Lord. [8] An indecisive man is unstable in all his ways.

[9] The brother of humble circumstances should boast in his exaltation; [10] but the one who is rich [should boast] in his humiliation, because he will pass away like a flower of the field. [11] For the sun rises with its scorching heat and dries up the grass; its flower falls off, and its beautiful appearance is destroyed. In the same way, the rich man will wither away while pursuing his activities.

[12] Blessed is a man who endures trials, because when he passes the test he will receive the crown of life that He has promised to those who love Him.

Life 101

3. True of False: Every believer experiences hardship.

4. You may not be required to _____ your _____ for God, but as a
   Christian you are required to _____ your _____ for Him.

Turning to God for Help

5. What three reasons make it necessary for you to seek God's help in dealing with
   life's struggles?
   1.
   2.
   3.

6. How can you get the wisdom to endure trials?

7. When you act on God's wisdom, you move from _____ to _____.

8. What two things will happen when you begin to rely on God's wisdom?
   1.
   2.

SMALL-GROUP TIME:
Small-group leaders will direct your discussions. Everyone will gain more if you are open and honest with your uncertainties and responses to questions.

 Do What? *(15 MINUTES)*

Group Experience: Wisdom Please

1. Which of the following most tests your faith?
   ☐ Friends
   ☐ School
   ☐ Parents
   ☐ Personal weaknesses
   ☐ Tests
   ☐ Your health
   ☐ Other: _____

2. What is your usual attitude toward the bad things that come your way? Are you pretty optimistic or terribly pessimistic? Does your attitude tend to rub off on others?

3. What are you going through right now in which you really need God's wisdom?

12

Making the critical decisions amidst life's adversities requires a wisdom unavailable by any means other than God.

These "Do" Points will help you grab hold of this week's LifePoint. Be open and honest as you answer the questions within your small group.

1. Stop trusting in worldly wisdom. Anything the world has to offer will be temporary and will always fall short of God's best for you.
   Why do you sometimes look to talk show hosts, un-Christian friends, and magazines for answers?

2. Ask God for wisdom. God truly does love it when you ask Him for something—especially something like wisdom.
   How easy is it for you to ask God for things? Why don't you ask Him more than you do?

3. Utilize Scripture's wisdom. From the Bible's first page to its last, you will find words to live by.
   What verses have you memorized that provide wisdom for dealing with tough times?

Prayer Connection:

This is the time to encourage, support, and pray for each other as you trust in God's wisdom to guide you individually and as a group.

Share prayer needs with the group, especially those related to relying on God. Your group facilitator will close your time in prayer.

Prayer Needs:

Remember your "Get Ready" daily Bible readings and questions at the beginning of Session 13 (the last session in this study).

 # now What?

Take it to the next level by completing the "Now What?" assignment this week:

List things in life that give you trouble. What are the greatest hardships you face? Put a mark beside the ones you believe God has already provided you the wisdom to handle. Circle the things for which you need to seek God's wisdom. Spend time this week asking God to help you get victory over the difficulties facing you.

12

Bible Reference Notes

Use these notes to deepen your understanding as you study the Bible on your own:

James 1:1   *James.* "James" is probably the half-brother of Jesus who was known in the early church as "James the Just."
a servant. Here he identifies Jesus as the "Lord" (master), therefore the appropriate relationship of all others to Jesus is as servants (literally "slaves").
the twelve tribes. In the New Testament, this came to be associated with the Christian church. Christians saw themselves as the new Israel (Rom. 4; 9:24–26; Phil. 3:3; 1 Peter 2:9–10).
scattered. The word is, literally, *diaspora* and was used by the Jews to refer to those of their number living outside of Israel in the Gentile world. Here it probably refers to those Jewish Christians living outside Israel (see 1 Peter 1:1).

James 1:2   *Consider it pure joy.* The joy James is talking about is not just a feeling. It is an active acceptance of adversity.
trials of many kinds. The word "trials" has the dual sense of "adversity" (e.g., disease, persecution, tragedy) and "temptations" (e.g., lust, greed, trust in wealth).

James 1:3   *perseverance.* Or "endurance." It is used in the sense of active overcoming, rather than passive acceptance.

James 1:4   *finish its work.* Perfection is not automatic—it takes time and effort.
mature and complete. What James has in mind here is wholeness of character.
lacking. The opposite of mature and complete. This is a word used of an army that has been defeated or a person who has failed to reach a certain standard.

James 1:5   *wisdom.* This is not just abstract knowledge, but God-given insight that leads to right living.

James 1:6   James now contrasts the readiness on God's part to give (v. 5) with the hesitation on people's part to ask (v. 6). Both here and in James 4:3, unanswered prayer is connected to the quality of the asking, not to the unwillingness of God to give.
believe. To be one in mind about God's ability to answer prayer.

James 1:8   *double-minded.* To doubt is to be in two minds—to believe and to disbelieve.

James 1:9   *The brother in humble circumstances.* This refers to those who are poor in a material and social sense and who are looked down on by others because they are poor.
take pride. This becomes possible when the poor see beyond immediate circumstances to their new position as children of God.
high position. In the early church, the poor gained a new sense of self-respect.

James 1:10   *rich.* The peril of riches is that people come to trust in wealth as a source of security.
low position. Jewish culture considered wealth to be a sign of God's favor. Here, as elsewhere (vv. 2,9), James reverses conventional "wisdom."

James 1:11   *scorching heat.* The hot, southeast desert wind (the *sirocco*) sweeps into Israel in the spring "like a blast of hot air when an oven door is opened."
fade away. Wealth gives an uncertain security, since it is apt to be swept away as abruptly as desert flowers (Isa. 40:6–8).

James 1:12   *Blessed.* Happy is the person who has withstood all the trials to the end.
stood the test. Such a person is like metal that has been purged by fire and is purified of all foreign substances.
crown of life. Crowns were worn at weddings and feasts (and so signify joy); they were also given to the winner of an athletic competition (and so signify victory); and were worn by royalty (as befits children of God the King).

13

GROWING THROUGH ADVERSITY

Get Ready

Spend a few moments getting to know God. Read one of these brief passages each day, and be sure to write down anything He reveals to you.

MONDAY

Read James 4:13-14

Do you dream about what you will do next week, next year, or ten years from now? Are you living in the present or in the future? What might result from putting too much of your energy into what might happen down the road?

TUESDAY

Read James 4:15

Why is it important to include God into your planning? In planning the future, what assumptions are you counting on?

WEDNESDAY

Read James 4:16

In what ways could our planning be arrogant? In what ways could we be accused of being boastful as we proclaim our visions?

13

THURSDAY

Read James 4:17

Have you ever missed an opportunity to do something good? Were you disappointed when you realized you'd missed it, or did you never intend to take the opportunity in the first place?

FRIDAY

Read Ephesians 5:15

How consistent are you in your relationship with the Lord? Would someone be able to easily recognize you as a Christian?

SATURDAY

Read Ephesians 5:16

Do you enjoy each day to the fullest? If you knew Jesus was coming back tomorrow, how would you spend this afternoon?

SUNDAY

Read Ephesians 5:17

What's the most foolish thing you could do in one day? What keeps you from doing it?

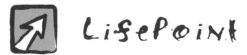 LifePoint

When your relationship with God is truly top priority, it is evident in how you decide to invest your time.

SMALL-GROUP
TIME:
Divide into
smaller groups of
4-8, preferably in
a circle. You will
have a small-
group leader for
"Say What?"

Say What? *(15 MINUTES)*

Random Question of the Week:
Starfish can regrow missing arms. Why can't people?

Group Experience: Which Piece Do You Want?
1. What do you spend most of your time doing?

2. If you could add four more hours to your day, how would you spend them?

3. How much of your day is spent learning about God's plan for you, talking to God, or doing something for Him?

So What? *(30 MINUTES)*

The Clock Is Ticking

1. How important is time to your relationship with God?

2. What was one thing that made Nehemiah a great man of God?

Learning from the Bible

¹³ Come now, you who say, "Today or tomorrow we will travel to such and such a city and spend a year there and do business and make a profit." ¹⁴ You don't even know what tomorrow will bring—what your life will be! For you are a bit of smoke that appears for a little while, then vanishes.

¹⁵ Instead, you should say, "If the Lord wills, we will live and do this or that." ¹⁶ But as it is, you boast in your arrogance. All such boasting is evil. ¹⁷ So, for the person who knows to do good and doesn't do it, it is a sin.

Managing Your Time

3. What one thing does everyone have in common?

4. According to the Bible, what is the wisest investment of time?

5. Which of the following resources cannot be replaced?

☐ Water
☐ Electricity
☐ Time
☐ Solar power
☐ Gasoline

Mismanaging Your Time

6. List three ways you can mismanage time:

1.

2.

3.

7. What is the problem with waiting to do something for God?

SMALL-GROUP TIME: Small-group leaders will direct your discussions. Everyone will gain more if you are open and honest in responding to questions.

 Do What? *(15 MINUTES)*

Group Experience: Can I see your ID, please?

1. Which of the following plans do you tend to leave God out of?

☐ Planning your calendar
☐ Picking the places where you will go
☐ Planning your future
☐ Doing the things you always do
☐ Deciding how to spend your money
☐ Other: _____

13

2. What would you like people to say about you at your funeral?

3. What are you are putting off until later, though you know God wants you to do it now? What adjustments will you need to make in order to do what God has called you to do?

LIFEPOINT
REVIEW

When your relationship with God is truly top priority, it is evident in how you decide to invest your time.

"DO" POINTS

These "Do" Points will help you grab hold of this week's LifePoint. Be open and honest as you answer the questions within your small group.

1. Write a personal mission statement that reflects God's priorities. Write it in broad terms that reflect God's purposes for your life and how you will accomplish them. **Have you ever written a personal mission statement? If so, how will this mission statement differ from those written previously?**

2. Pray during your personal planning process. Sit down and plan your week, including your daily schedule, classes, practices, and special appointments. **How can you honor God in through this week's activities?**

3. Obey God by doing what He has led you to do. God is always at work in your life. He is always calling you to serve Him in some new and exciting way. **What did God last ask of you? Have you obeyed Him?**

Prayer Connection:

This is the time to encourage, support, and pray for each other as continue to develop a deeper understanding of God's mysterious, complex character.

Share prayer needs with the group, especially those related to how you are investing your time. Your group facilitator will close your time in prayer.

Prayer Needs:

Even though you have finished this study. These "Now What?" assignments will help you to really experience grace.

It will help to go back and review your notes from this study over the next couple of weeks.

 now What?

Take it to the next level by completing one of these assignments this week:

Option #1:

Post a weekly calendar in your locker or room. On every day of the week, include a plan—no matter how simple it might seem—to do something specific for God. Before attempting to carry out any of those plans, make sure you are trying to accomplish the things God wants you to do rather those you choose for yourself.

Option #2:

Make a poster with the heading, "The Most." As you meditate on God's Word this week, list on the poster all the ways you can make the most of each day for God. Search Scripture for ideas and include your own.

13

Bible Reference Notes

Use these notes to deepen your understanding as you study the Bible on your own:

James 4:13   Boasting about the future is arrogant because God is the only one who knows what will happen in the future.

Today or tomorrow we will go. In trade, a person in the first century had to plan ahead. Travel plans, market projections, time frames, and profit forecasts are the stuff of business in all ages. Every honest merchant would plan in exactly the same way—pagan, Jew, or Christian—and that is exactly the problem James has with these plans: There is absolutely nothing about their desires for the future, their use of money, or their way of doing business that is any different from the rest of the world.

carry on business. The word James uses here is from the Greek word *emporos*, from which the English word "emporium" comes. It denotes wholesale merchants who traveled from city to city, buying and selling.

James 4:14   *tomorrow.* All such planning presupposes that tomorrow will unfold like any other day, when, in fact, the future is anything but secure (see Prov. 27:1).

What is your life? Is not death the great unknown? Who can know when death will come? By thinking on the worldly plane, the Christian business people James addressed have gained a false sense of security. They need to look death in the face and realize their lack of control over life.

mist. Hosea 13:3 says, "Therefore they will be like the morning mist, like the early dew that disappears, like chaff swirling from a threshing floor, like smoke escaping through a window."

James 4:15   *If it is the Lord's will.* The uncertainty of the future ought not to be a terror to the Christian. Instead, it ought to force an awareness of how dependent a person is upon God, and thus move that person to a planning structure that involves God.

we will live and do this or that. James is not ruling out planning. He says plan, but keep God in mind.

James 4:16   *boast.* The problem with this boasting is that they are claiming to have the future under control when, in fact, it is God who holds time in His hands.

brag. This word originally described an itinerant quack who touted "cures" that did not work. It came to mean claiming to be able to do something that you could not do.

Acknowledgments:

We sincerely appreciate the great team of people that worked to develop *Critical Decisions: Clarity in the Journey, Youth Edition.* Special thanks are extended to David Bennett for adapting the adult study and writing the student version. We also appreciate the editorial and production team that consisted of Brian Daniel, Brian Marschall, Joe Moore of Powell Creative, Bethany McShurley, and Jenna Anderson.

13

GROUP
DIRECTORY

NAME	PHONE	E-MAIL